TEACHERS' GUIDE TO SCHOOL TURNAROUNDS

Daniel L. Duke,
Pamela D. Tucker,
Michael J. Salmonowicz,
Melissa Levy,
and Stephen Saunders

Partnership for Leaders
in Education
University of Virginia

Rowman & Littlefield Education
Lanham • New York • Toronto • Plymouth, UK
2008

Published in the United States of America
by Rowman & Littlefield Education
A Division of Rowman & Littlefield Publishers, Inc.
A wholly owned subsidiary of The Rowman & Littlefield Publishing Group,
Inc.
4501 Forbes Boulevard, Suite 200, Lanham, Maryland 20706
www.rowmaneducation.com

Estover Road
Plymouth PL6 7PY
United Kingdom

British Library Cataloguing in Publication Information Available

Library of Congress Cataloging-in-Publication Data

Teachers' guide to school turnarounds / Daniel L. Duke . . . [et al.].
    p. cm.
  ISBN-13: 978-1-57886-667-0 (cloth : alk. paper)
  ISBN-10: 1-57886-667-7 (cloth : alk. paper)
  ISBN-13: 978-1-57886-668-7 (pbk. : alk. paper)
  ISBN-10: 1-57886-668-5 (pbk. : alk. paper)
    1. School improvement programs—United States—Handbooks, manuals, etc.
2. Educational change—United States—Handbooks, manuals, etc. I. Duke,
Daniel Linden.
  LB2822.82.T435 2008
  371.2—dc22   2007020819

Manufactured in the United States of America.

Acknowledgements

The authors would like to express their appreciation to the Microsoft Corporation for its generous support of this project.

The following teachers provided invaluable input for this book: Margie Badgett-Lampkin, Lena Chambers, Chris Dianas, Laura Funk, Malina Gaynor, Peggy Howard, Anna Marie Jasko, Melissa Jefferson, Sharyn Kauffman, Lola Vann McDowell, Natasha M. Richmond, Hilary Siegrist, Clover Willis, Jane Willis, Katrina Wilson, and Margaret P. Wooding. They are to be commended for their efforts to turn around low-performing schools.

Contents

1

It Takes a Faculty to Turn around a School

Graduation day at Jefferson High School. Randall Jones stands when his name is called and strides confidently across the stage, shakes the principal's hand, and accepts the diploma that many people doubted he would ever receive. Hadn't he struggled with reading when he was a child? Didn't he miss more than his share of classes in middle school? Wasn't his mother worried he might fall in with the wrong crowd in high school? Yet there he was, a high school graduate with a generous scholarship to a fine college.

Whose hands were clapping loudest for Randall as he turned briefly and smiled at the audience? Probably it was Randall's mother, but it also could have been his second-grade reading teacher who helped him with word recognition during her lunch period, his middle school counselor who phoned home every day that Randall was absent, his high school basketball coach and social studies teacher who made certain Randall stayed too busy to pick up bad habits, or any one of dozens of other educators who did whatever they could to keep Randall's eyes on the prize.

The fact is that no young person succeeds in getting an education without the contributions of a small army of trained professionals. Similarly, it is impossible to turn around a low-performing school without the expertise and active involvement of the faculty. Leaders attract lots of attention and capture the headlines, but no principal or "school turnaround specialist" can singlehandedly reverse a school's downward slide, nor can a superintendent or team of central office specialists. Even a cadre of concerned parents and community volunteers is unlikely to be up to the challenge. Good intentions simply are not enough to improve school performance. It takes a competent and committed faculty to turn around a school.

This book is first and foremost for teachers, especially teachers who are engaged in, or are getting ready to engage in, the process of improving a low-performing school. The central message of the book is deceptively simple. It can be done! Low-performing schools can be turned around. But not without you.

In the pages to follow, we will share what we have been learning from educators involved in turning around low-performing schools. While some of this knowledge is secondhand, gleaned from excellent case studies of successful school improvement projects, most of what we present is based on firsthand knowledge, the result of our fieldwork and conversations with educators participating in the School Turnaround Specialist Program at the University of Virginia. This program has worked with low-performing schools across the United States to create conditions conducive to effective teaching and productive learning. The results, as you will see later in the book, have been heartening.

In order to prepare you for the challenges of the school turnaround process, we believe that you can benefit from reflecting on several questions:

- What conditions contribute to low performance in schools?
- What can teachers do individually and collectively to overcome these conditions?
- Once student achievement has been raised, what can be done to sustain success?
- How is participation in the school turnaround process likely to affect teachers?

Each of these questions will be addressed in this book.

WHY THE INTEREST IN SCHOOL TURNAROUNDS?

Interest in school improvement has existed since the beginning of formal schooling, but there is reason to believe that the focus on turning around low-performing schools has never been as intense as it is today. As a result of the landmark No Child Left Behind Act and various accountability initiatives in virtually every state in the United States, schools now face serious sanctions if they fail to meet designated achievement benchmarks. Schools that fail to meet adequate yearly progress under No Child Left Behind, for example, may be subject to the following actions:

- Reopening as a public charter school.
- Replacing "all or most of the school staff (which may include the principal) who are relevant to the failure to make adequate yearly progress."
- Contracting with "an outside entity, such as a private management company, with a demonstrated record of effectiveness, to operate the school."
- Turning the "operation of the school over to the state educational agency, if permitted under State law and agreed to by the State."
- Engaging in another form of major restructuring that makes fundamental reforms, "such as significant changes in the school's staffing and governance, to improve student academic achievement in the school and that has substantial promise of enabling the school to make adequate yearly progress." (No Child Left Behind Act 2002).

Before No Child Left Behind, a school may have been required to develop an annual school improvement plan with specific goals for raising student achievement and addressing other issues facing the school, but these plans were not always monitored very closely. Sometimes the very teachers expected to implement the plan knew very little of its contents. The plan may have been regarded by the administration as one of a seemingly endless number of bureaucratic activities that, once undertaken, were soon forgotten.

No longer is it possible to treat school improvement in such a cavalier fashion. The reason is as clear as a kindergartner's complexion. Too much in a young person's life depends on how well they do in school. While school success cannot guarantee success in life, school failure is a reliable predictor of future failure. We must do *everything* in our power as professionals to ensure that every child attains a quality education. This may mean, under certain circumstances, that a low-performing school must undergo a "turnaround" process.

WHEN IS A SCHOOL "TURNED AROUND"?

When a business is failing, it often loses customers. So, too, with low-performing schools. Teachers watch helplessly as parents withdraw their children and enroll them in other schools. Sometimes parents even opt for homeschooling in an effort to improve their child's chances of academic success. One indication that a school is turning around, therefore, could be the return of once-disaffected parents and increasing enrollment.

The No Child Left Behind Act specifies that the turnaround process begins when the leadership of a school district elects the so-called restructuring option for a chronically low-performing school. This option entails replacing the principal and some or all of the staff.

In the School Turnaround Specialist Program with which we are associated, a school achieves the first stage of the turnaround process when it raises student achievement on state standardized tests to a point where it achieves (1) adequate yearly progress under No Child Left Behind, (2) accreditation under the guidelines of the state's standards of accreditation, or (3) "safe harbor" (represented by a 10 percent reduction in the number of students failing state tests in reading or mathematics). Of particular importance with these criteria is evidence that the gap in achievement between white and minority students is decreasing.

As you doubtless have surmised, there is no single, agreed-upon basis for determining that a school has turned around. As for the term "school turnaround," it is simply the descendent of such prior terms as "school improvement" and "school restructuring." "Turnaround" connotes that a period of low achievement has come to an end and initial indications of improving achievement are in evidence. Improvement, of course, depends ultimately on whether initial success can be sustained over time.

In order to achieve school turnarounds, various states are implementing an array of special initiatives, ranging from dispatching specially trained assistance teams to pairing low-performing schools with high-performing schools. Some states have concentrated primarily on school leadership, training "school turnaround specialists," and pairing principals with veteran administrators. In virtually every state, teachers in low-performing schools are being provided with focused staff development. The days when low-performing schools were allowed to continue being low-performing schools are clearly over.

A word or two on the term "low-performing schools" is in order before we continue. We realize that a school does not perform. It is the teachers and students in a school who are responsible for accomplishing desired outcomes. We use the term "low-performing school" as a shorthand reference for a school where teachers and students are not achieving desired outcomes. There are many reasons for low performance, and these reasons will be explored in chapter 3.

A FEW WORDS ABOUT THE AUTHORS

We realize that credibility is important when professional educators receive advice from others. While we do not presume to match the collective wisdom of a faculty regarding the conditions in their school, we have studied many schools in various locations and therefore are in a position to offer an extensive overview of school turnaround efforts that may be unavailable locally. Each of us has been a public school teacher, and the two senior authors have been school administrators. While our experience as practitioners has been invaluable, the insights and understandings that have proven most valuable in preparing this book have come from listening to educators like yourselves who have faced and are facing the challenges of turning around low-performing schools. Over the past four years, we have conducted a dozen studies on the school turnaround process. This work has been made possible in large part by generous funding from the Microsoft Corporation. In addition, we have consulted the work of other researchers engaged in the study of what it takes to turn around low-performing schools. It is our sincerest hope that this book will serve as a catalyst to productive discussions among you and your colleagues about the best ways to raise student achievement in your school. If our information can save you and your school a "false start," a well-intentioned but misdirected reform, or a "blindside" unwanted surprise, we will be pleased. If we can contribute to more productive teaching and learning in your school, we will be elated.

OVERVIEW OF THE BOOK

When we are in the midst of a difficult situation, we are not always able to see clearly how to correct it. It is all we can do just to cope. Under such daunting circumstances, a positive example can serve as a beacon of hope. We follow this chapter, therefore, with a case study of a low-performing school that overcame tremendous odds in the process of rising from the ashes. The heartening story of this school turnaround is not a fluke, as the second part of chapter 2 reveals. A substantial number of public schools in the United States have been able to escape the gravitational pull of poverty, neglect, and low performance.

Why some schools are less successful than other schools is a matter of considerable debate. It seems that everyone has an opinion on the subject. It is our contention that significant progress on school improvement is unlikely until teachers, principals, and parents examine their explanations for low performance. Each explanation leads to a particular corrective strategy. When people disagree about the causes of low performance, they also are apt to disagree about how to correct it. Chapter 3 explores the variety of explanations that have been offered to account for lack of school success. Among the many factors that can contribute to low performance in school is one that strikes close to home. Teachers' beliefs and behavior cannot be overlooked when searching for explanations. If teachers deserve credit for student success, they also must be prepared to "own" some responsibility for student failure. So critical are the matters of teacher competence, concern, and commitment that we devoted the last part of chapter 3 to looking at the relationship between how teachers think, how teachers act, and how students learn.

In order to undertake the process of turning around a low-performing school, it is necessary to closely examine the conditions in the school that may be holding down performance. This examination is analogous to diagnosing a medical problem. The goal is to determine the "health" of the school and the course of action necessary to address any health problems. Chapter 4 discusses various sources of data on school conditions, including achievement indicators, student data, and information on instruction, school organization, and school culture.

Once a thorough and honest assessment of school conditions has been undertaken, teachers and administrators need to draw on the findings and plan a series of steps leading to improved performance. Chapter 5 focuses on the planning required to launch a school turnaround initiative. Planning begins with determining a school's "capacity for change" and continues with efforts to define priorities, evaluate faculty readiness, and decide whether or not to adopt an established school improvement program.

The ultimate success of school turnaround initiatives can depend on the actions educators take to begin the process. Low-performing schools often are characterized by a variety of challenging conditions. Depending on available expertise and resources, it may not be wise to tackle every condition immediately. Successful school turnarounds frequently focus on several key reforms in order to launch the process. Chapter 6 describes what might be expected to occur during the early stages of the school turnaround process and the responsibilities that teachers may be expected to assume.

The advice in chapter 6 can help you to get your school turnaround off on the right foot. How to sustain that initial success is the focus of chapter 7. We draw on the experiences of former low-performing public schools that overcame numerous obstacles in the course of raising student achievement and keeping it raised. Chapter 7 addresses the roles that teachers should be prepared to play in order to maintain an effective learning environment. Also discussed are the contributions of students, parents, principals, and the central office to sustained school success.

The penultimate chapter provides an opportunity to reflect on the challenges of change. Relying on the experiences of educators who have participated in the school turnaround process, we examine some of the ways change can impact teachers personally and professionally. By forewarning you about these possible impacts, we hope to eliminate any unwanted surprises and alert you about what to expect when you embark on the journey to a better school.

Every teacher who engages in the process of turning around a low-performing school can use some help. If we had covered all the possible sources of assistance in depth, this book would have swelled to a length that might have discouraged readers. Instead, we chose to summarize various resources available to "turnaround teachers" in the final chapter. Chapter 9 includes sources for case studies of school turnarounds, instruments that can be used to assess school conditions, and other sources of relevant information, including websites.

To enhance the value and readability of this book, we employ several editorial devices. Each chapter, for example, contains several "key questions." These questions serve as a focus for our sharing of information, but they also are intended as a possible prompt for discussions among you and your colleagues. Throughout the book, you also will find various "turnaround tips" and "turnaround traps" set off from the text. These tips and traps constitute abbreviated versions of the advice available in the book. At the end of each chapter, we provide several suggestions for things that you and your colleagues can do as a follow-up. We believe that reading and discussing this book with your fellow teachers and undertaking the follow-up activities will prepare you for the challenges of school turn-around.

2

School Turnaround Is Not a Myth

The need for school turnaround has never been greater. Under No Child Left Behind, the percentage of students who are expected to pass state assessments increases each successive year with the ultimate goal of 100 percent by 2014. As the demands increase, more schools are failing to meet adequate yearly progress (AYP). In the 2005–2006 school year, 29 percent of all schools failed to make AYP, an increase of 4 percentage points over the previous year. That's close to twenty-two thousand schools nationwide where an insufficient number of children are learning at a level considered reasonable by state officials. These are schools whose children need caring and committed educators to take collective responsibility for teaching and learning in their buildings and create a better future for their students.

Ron Edmonds, father of the Effective Schools Research, asked the pointed question, "How many effective schools would you have to see to be persuaded of the educability of poor children?" Edmonds's research objective thirty years ago was to identify as many high-poverty, high-performing schools as necessary to satisfy those who were doubtful, and his work remains relevant today. In this chapter, we examine several schools that have been turned around and have become effective in serving challenging student populations. We begin with a discussion of the turnaround dynamics of one school in some detail and continue with several others in thumbnail sketches. While every school has a unique set of challenges and circumstances, we have found the problems facing low-performing schools are typically substantial and complex like those in the following case.

> *Turnaround Thought:* The question is not, "Is it possible to educate all children well?" but rather, "Do we want to do it badly enough?" (Deborah Meier)

GREENFIELD ELEMENTARY SCHOOL

Before Greenfield Elementary School began the turnaround process three years ago, it had similarities with many underperforming Title I schools in the United States. Despite low test scores, there was a core of committed, hardworking teachers and a multitude of energetic, curious students. Over a third of the children qualified for free or reduced-price lunch and most came from families of modest means. The rural, working-class community trusted the school to take care of its children and was generally supportive. The specific causes of the school's downward spiral were unclear, but declining test scores were a clear indication of problems within the school. Teachers were miserable and the culture of the school was described as a toxic one in which the focus had shifted from the needs of children to the concerns of adults. There was no collective purpose or goal for teaching and educators worked in isolation, interacting with each other as little as possible. Greenfield had lost direction and become an island of neglect.

Harsh Realities

In 2004, only 32 percent of the third graders in this school of three hundred fifty passed the state reading assessment, and worse yet, only 8 percent of the third-grade students with disabilities passed it. Almost a fifth (18%) of the students at Greenfield were identified for special education services, above the percentage of special education students at most schools. Increasing numbers of children were failing their assessments across all grade levels and content areas. Greenfield was the *only* school in a district of twenty-eight schools to be accredited with warning. All other schools were fully accredited. In addition, Greenfield did not make

AYP for the 2003–2004 or 2004–2005 school years. Based on sanctions under No Child Left Behind, the school was declared to be in the first year of school improvement, and it was designated a school of choice for the 2004–2005 school year. This meant that parents could choose to send their children to other schools in the district and transportation would be provided for them. The families of eleven children opted to exercise this option in September 2004.

The testing results and state sanctions were a wake-up call to the school district, which began exploring options for bringing about improvements at the school. As a first step, a new principal was hired for the 2004–2005 school year and given the clear mandate from the central office to reverse the downward trend at Greenfield. Sara Jamison, a participant in the School Turnaround Specialist Program, was that principal. The School Turnaround Program provided Jamison with advanced training and coaching in how to undertake and assess improvement in low-performing schools. The program stresses the development of school-based leadership teams, reflecting the fact that one lone individual cannot effect organizational change. The ultimate success of Greenfield Elementary School is attributable to the commitment and hard work of the faculty members who stepped forward to bring about change through collaboration, professional development, and their common concern for children. Some teachers served on the leadership team, which represented all subject areas and grade levels in the school, while others provided support and encouragement as grade-level or subject-area team members. It was this network of engaged individuals that made the difference between stagnation and movement forward.

Table 2.1. Profile of Greenfield Elementary School

Student Enrollment	352
Percent of Economically Disadvantaged Students	33
Percent of Students with Disabilities	18
State Accreditation Status	Accredited w/warning
Adequate Yearly Progress Status	Did Not Make AYP
Percent of Students Proficient on State Reading Test	
Grade 3	32
Grade 5	64
Percent of Students Proficient on State Math Test	
Grade 3	71
Grade 5	42

The extent of the neglect that Ms. Jamison found upon arriving at Greenfield was palpable. There were no formalized committees in place, no written plans of any kind, and no defined instructional plan. The building was in physical disrepair. The finances were being audited, and the school was developing a negative reputation in the community. Parent and business support was being withdrawn. The most fundamental challenge facing the new principal, however, was the negative culture that had developed in the school. Due to internal struggles among the faculty and the former principal, people were emotionally raw. The Greenfield staff included many inexperienced teachers as well as some veteran teachers who had given up hope for student success. So complete was the preoccupation with adult issues in the school that teachers were unaware of Greenfield's accreditation and AYP status until the new principal informed them upon their return to school in August 2004.

New Beginnings

Before the school year even started, Ms. Jamison identified Greenfield's key instructional leaders, and those with leadership potential, and invited them to participate in a two-day retreat to begin the planning process for the year. Each grade level was represented as well as the support services, Title I, and special education. Over the course of those two days, participants shared their frustrations, then refocused on the future and articulated inspiring vision and mission statements for the school. The group began to build relationships and a collective commitment to creating a positive learning environment for students at Greenfield. They adopted the motto: "Creating Success—No Exceptions, No Excuses."

The retreat was just the first of a series of efforts by the principal to both heal the wounds of the past and push teachers to acknowledge the need for change. During the first workweek with teachers, Jamison introduced the idea of professional learning communities as a means to examine the existing needs of children in the school and establish improvement goals. The three fundamental questions that drive a professional learning community are

1. What do we want each student to learn?
2. How will we know when each student has learned it?

3. How will we respond when a student experiences difficulty in learning? (DuFour, Eaker, and DuFour 2005).

With these questions as the organizing framework for their discussions, teachers began to examine existing curriculum, instruction, and assessment at the school.

The day before classes started, the principal and teachers developed a collaborative plan of action for the year. The plan addressed many problems identified by the teachers, such as the lack of a reasonable master schedule, support services (Title I, special education, etc.), instructional materials, updated curriculum guides, staff development focused on reading instruction, and better attendance by students. None of the problems was resolved, but teachers had identified the barriers that they felt were hampering their efforts to serve children.

Once the school year began, the staff conducted subject-by-subject program evaluations to identify what was working and not working based on teachers' experiences. As a part of this work, Jamison found that teachers were unaware of the school's performance on state testing, and a whole workday subsequently was spent reviewing test data from the previous three years. Teachers analyzed the data to better understand program effectiveness and identify instructional weaknesses. This information then was used to set specific targets for student achievement by grade level. The principal was heartened to find that a driving question from teachers was "Where do we need to improve to be fully accredited?" It was this kind of teacher concern and commitment that provided forward momentum despite the anxious mood that characterized the school during the first few months.

The leadership team continued to meet every week to discuss the status of various projects and interventions and to make decisions on schoolwide issues. Each team member was responsible for disseminating information to colleagues in grade-level or special team meetings (Title I, special education, arts and physical education, etc.). They also were expected to share concerns of the various teams with the leadership team to provide a constant stream of two-way communication. Grade-level teams met every two weeks to discuss curriculum and formative assessments of student learning. Benchmark testing became an important instructional feedback mechanism that was used to make ongoing curriculum adjustments.

Not everyone, however, was on board with the changes taking place. There were numerous personnel problems involving teachers who were unable or unwilling to collaborate with their colleagues on improvement efforts. In previous years, low-performing teachers from other schools had been allowed to transfer to Greenfield, and some of these teachers were resistant to the new expectations. With Jamison's arrival, several struggling teachers left the school; others were reassigned or placed on plans of assistance. Specialists were placed strategically in content areas or grade levels to compensate for potentially weak instruction.

The principal advocated for additional resources in a number of areas for the school. Requests for new instructional materials such as math manipulatives, up-to-date maps and globes, and more textbooks were granted by the central office. Intensive, job-embedded professional development on reading and literacy was provided to all teachers. Support personnel in the central office assisted the principal in addressing chronic attendance problems with identified families. Lastly, the central office approved a benchmark testing program to provide frequent feedback to teachers on student mastery of content in the core subject areas.

Teachers were initially hesitant about the use of benchmark testing, but the principal convinced them of its utility as a tool for making instructional adjustments during the course of the year. Jamison set up a school database tracking system for all student information, including past testing, with easy access for teachers. The first benchmark test results in November were very low and disheartening, but they confirmed the urgency for the types of changes that were being made. The results of the second set of benchmark tests, given in January, were awaited with great anticipation by both students and teachers. Even parents called the school to see what effect the changes were making on student learning. The second round of benchmark test scores were much higher than the first, engendering more positive conversations among teachers about teaching and learning.

> *Turnaround Tip:* For any change process, it is essential to have concrete evidence of success early in the process to encourage ongoing efforts to accomplish stated goals.

As a result of the early indicators of improvement, the general mood at Greenfield became more energized and upbeat in the spring. There were

Friday afternoon faculty get-togethers to play volleyball and floor hockey. Teachers began laughing and having fun together. They were collaborating within and across grade-level teams to a greater extent. The focus was squarely on children and their academic needs. The school was becoming a professional learning community that was goal-driven and actively pursuing new knowledge to better inform instruction. The third round of benchmark testing in March confirmed earlier progress and helped to identify areas for additional attention and review in anticipation of end-of-year state testing. Jamison and the teachers were hopeful that their focused efforts to align and supplement the curriculum, monitor instruction, and enhance their instructional skills would reap positive results.

Promising Outcomes

After a challenging year of changes in almost every aspect of the school, the percentage of students passing the state assessments rose in every area except one. In third-grade English, the percentage of students passing climbed from 32 percent to 61 percent, and in fifth grade, the percentage rose from 64 percent to 71 percent. In math, the percentage of students passing in third grade went up fifteen points and in fifth grade it increased twenty-seven points. As a result, Greenfield made AYP and was fully accredited by the state in 2005–2006. The school had been successful in improving student achievement and most teachers were excited and eager to start the second year of turnaround.

The teachers and principal experienced year two as far more fun and exciting. The leadership team and the faculty worked to formalize the changes that were initiated in the first year. Teachers had a newfound sense of confidence about their ability to meet academic targets for state accreditation and AYP. They had a better sense of how to work together in teams, design curriculum, and intervene with struggling students. While Greenfield teachers had not reached their goal of 90 percent of students reading on grade level, they were making substantial gains and were energized by the successes of the first year. The second year offered the opportunity to hire new faculty, refine the curriculum, and realign resources to support the primary goal of reading.

Thirteen teachers left during the 2005–2006 school year. Their replacements elevated the energy level in the building. Some of the new teachers were novices, but others were experienced teachers from within and out-side of the school district. It was especially encouraging to the leadership team that teachers from within the school district were willing to request transfers to Greenfield. The leadership team organized an intensive teacher preparation program the week before school started to enable the newcomers to hit the ground running with an understanding of the newly developed reading and math curricula, data analysis skills, and an appreciation for the team spirit within the school.

> *Turnaround Tip:* The process of change can be unsettling to some faculty. The resulting staff turnover may be a normal part of reshaping a school's culture.

In the second year, reading continued to be a primary focus for improvement efforts and resources were aligned to support that goal. Teachers had developed and implemented a new reading curriculum in the first year, but it was not until the following summer that a group of interested teachers committed to paper the formal reading and writing program for the school. Notebooks were developed and norms were established about how reading was to be taught in the building. Teachers also researched effective instructional strategies for reading and then provided in-service workshops on how to deliver effective guided reading instruction, diagnose reading difficulties, and implement appropriate and effective interventions for struggling readers. Staff meetings were opportunities for teachers to teach colleagues. A heavy emphasis was placed on reading, and instruction often was delivered by the reading team. Instructional funds were spent to purchase books for both the school library and classroom libraries. Reading was clearly the number one priority, and everyone in the building was mobilized around the goal of improving reading achievement.

Another area of concern, special education, became the focus of program evaluation during the second year. There were numerous problems with special education: disproportionately large numbers of students were identified for services, students who were receiving services lacked adequate paperwork and documentation of testing, and a majority of special education students failed the state and alternative assessments in English and math. The principal turned to the central office and solicited the coordinator of special education's support in the review of all the existing Individualized Education Plans (IEPs) and evaluation of the entire special education program at Greenfield. Two new special educators were hired to build a team charged with overhauling the program for students with disabilities. Teachers were sent to conferences to learn about collaborative teaching. With the assistance of the special education coordinator, they developed a new model of instruction for special education services.

> *Turnaround Trap:* The school turnaround process can be overwhelmed by identifying too many goals and priorities for a given year. One overarching goal, such as reading proficiency for all children, may be better than ten lesser goals.

During the first year, Sara Jamison and Greenfield's teachers established a basic understanding about their goals and priorities, created a common vocabulary about teaching and learning, and began working together in more productive ways. They experimented with new curricula and teaching techniques. They began discussing student learning in a systematic manner that informed their instruction. They laid the foundation for school turnaround in the first year, but it was in the second year that they really began to consolidate their knowledge and skills, and build upon them to become even more effective in the classroom.

Maintaining momentum in the change process, however, can be challenging. Despite continuing efforts by teachers to improve the instructional program, less dramatic achievement results were realized in the second year. Greenfield improved again in third-grade English, rising from 61 percent to 69 percent of students passing the state assessment, but the percentage of students passing the other tests remained relatively constant and even dipped slightly in fifth-grade math. The fifth-grade team's ability to make the kind of gains they had hoped to make during the year was hampered by the unexpected medical leave of a teacher. Despite efforts to compensate for the missing team member, the fifth grade lost ground in math compared to the previous year.

> *Turnaround Tip:* Educators must persist through unexpected difficulties, setbacks, and failures.

Table 2.2.

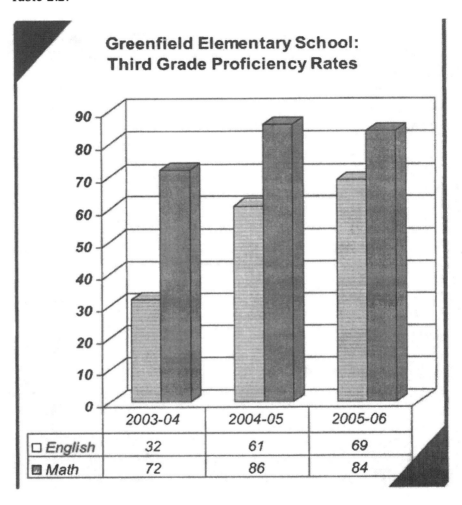

Greenfield Elementary School:
Third Grade Proficiency Rates

	2003-04	2004-05	2005-06
☐ English	32	61	69
▨ Math	72	86	84

Change theorists often stress that deep organizational change requires three to five years to take hold and that improvement is seldom a consistent upward trend. Setbacks and unexpected challenges are just part of the messy business of change. This was certainly true at Greenfield, though the first two years of turnaround were still promising, particularly in reading, which had been identified as the top priority by the leadership team. The teachers and students made tremendous strides, considering the chaos that had existed in the school prior to the arrival of Sara Jamison. Her role

Table 2.3.

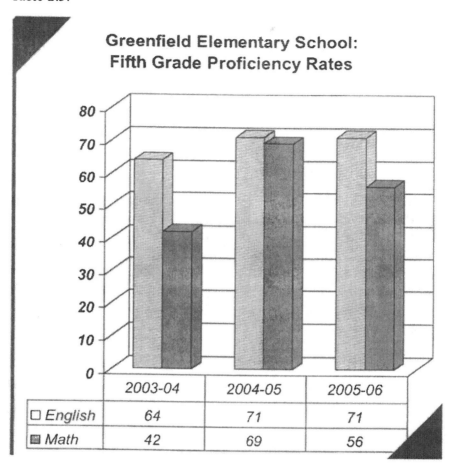

Greenfield Elementary School: Fifth Grade Proficiency Rates

	2003-04	2004-05	2005-06
☐ English	64	71	71
▨ Math	42	69	56

as principal was to remind the Greenfield faculty of why they had become teachers in the first place and then to support them as they collectively re-defined the academic program at Greenfield Elementary School.

OTHER EXAMPLES OF SCHOOL TURNAROUND

Concerted efforts by dedicated educators in other locations have brought about the same kinds of changes that took place at Greenfield Elementary School. These educators' stories have been told in research monographs, newspapers, and even the movies. Awards are now being given on an annual basis to schools that defy the odds in challenging circumstances and create islands of excellence for students. The power of teachers working together for the benefit of children, particularly low-income students and students of color, is unrivaled as a mechanism for educational change. The following are a few more examples of turnaround schools that serve a wide variety of students at different grade levels and in different parts of the country. Additional case studies of remarkable schools can be found in the references for this chapter and in chapter 9.

East Millsboro Elementary School (Millsboro, Delaware)

This elementary school enrolls about seven hundred students in grades preK through five in a rural part of Delaware.[1] Many of the adults in the community work in chicken-processing plants and their children qualify for free and reduced-price lunch (50%). The student body is predominantly Caucasian. Twenty-five percent of the students are African American and 13 percent are Latino, though the Latino population is a growing segment of the community. Over the past five years, the proficiency rates for both third and fifth graders in reading and math have inched up and hit the 94 to 95 percent level. These rates exceed the averages for the school district and the state and, in fact, are some of the highest in the state.

Stanton M. Hall Elementary School (Philadelphia, Pennsylvania)

Stanton M. Hall sits in a downtrodden neighborhood in North Philadelphia and serves 436 students in grades K through six. Students are 99.3 percent African-American and 99.3 percent economically disadvantaged. In the years between 2001 and 2003, fifth-grade proficiency rates in reading and math hovered below the 20 percent mark. Beginning in 2004, however, the school began a stunning turnaround and now boasts a 70 percent proficiency rate in reading and 83 percent proficiency rate in math at the fifth-grade level. These rates exceed both the school district and state averages.

---

[1]Data obtained from www.schoolmatters.com

Port Chester Middle School (Port Chester, New York)

Port Chester Middle School is situated in a poor, working-class neighborhood in wealthy Westchester County and serves approximately 750 students in grades five through eight. Hispanics make up 64 percent of the student body with another 24 percent Caucasian and 12 percent African American. With a longstanding reputation for poor academics and discipline, it had begun a slow but steady turnaround beginning in 2002 when eighth-grade proficiency rates were 56 percent in reading and 66 percent in math. Now, 68 percent of students are proficient in reading and 85 percent of the students are proficient in math, percentages that match the school district average and exceed the state average.

Elmont Memorial Junior-Senior High School (Elmont, New York)

Located on Long Island just across from Queens, Elmont Memorial Junior-Senior High School is a remarkable story of sustained achievement. A large brick building houses almost two thousand students in grades seven through twelve. Most students come from the working class neighborhoods that surround the school. The student population is largely minority, with the majority (75%) of the students being African American and 10 percent described as Hispanic. Roughly 20 percent of its students receive government assistance (either free or reduced-price lunch). Year after year, Elmont Memorial posts some of the highest student achievement scores in the state of New York. In 2005, for example, its entire senior class graduated, many with advanced diplomas, and 97 percent of this class went on to college.

Frederick Douglass Academy (New York, New York)

The Frederick Douglass Academy is located in central Harlem and serves approximately eight hundred students in grades eight through twelve. The neighborhood is very poor and predominately minority. The student population is 84 percent African American and 14 percent Hispanic. Despite proficiency rates of 50 to 60 percent for the eighth graders who are tested in their first year at the school, the school posted 97 percent proficiency rates in reading and 92 percent proficiency rates in math on the High School Regent's Exams for the 2004–2005 school year. The proficiency rates have been relatively high since the school was reconstituted back in 1991 and currently exceed the averages for New York City Public Schools and for the state.

Imperial High School (Imperial Valley, California)

Just a few miles from the Mexican border in southern California, Imperial High School serves grades nine through twelve and has a predominantly Latino student body (70%) with 27 percent Caucasian. Many of the Latino students are English Language Learners. One third of the students are classified as economically disadvantaged. In 2000, this school was considered low performing and had an Academic Performance Index of 621. By 2006, its Academic Performance Index had climbed to 785 on a scale of 800 (2006 median of 699). Proficiency rates on the English language arts and math tests ranged from 79 percent to 88 percent, exceeding the school district and state averages on all tests at all levels.

This sampling of schools from across the nation demonstrates that schools with poor and minority students can be successful. Their success, however, isn't a result of quick fixes; their success is the consequence of dedicated and excellent staff working hard to ensure that each student receives a quality education. All of these schools provide proof that any school, regardless of who its students are or where they live, can achieve at high academic levels. As noted by Kati Haycock of the Education Trust, "These schools should inspire us and challenge all of us to realize the potential in our public schools" (2006, 2).

LARGE SCALE NEED FOR ACTION

In 2004–2005, the same year that Sara Jamison was hired to turn around Greenfield Elementary School, 25 percent of the schools nationwide did not make AYP, and roughly half of those were deemed to be "in need of improvement" due to consistent low performance. Some states had much lower percentages of schools not making AYP. Only 4 percent of Wisconsin's schools, for example, did not meet the performance standards. Other places, such as the District of Columbia, had much higher percentages of schools not meeting AYP (85%). Possibly due to the annual increases in the percentages of students who were required to pass state assessments each consecutive year, there was a four-point increase in the percentage of schools not making AYP in 2005–2006.

Given the numerous reporting requirements of No Child Left Behind, there are often examples of schools that failed to meet AYP simply because of a single subgroup of children who did not pass a given test. In reality, only 23 percent of schools that failed to meet AYP in 2003–2004 did so because of the low achievement of a single subgroup. More common (33% of schools that failed to make AYP) was the inability of schools to meet AYP requirements due to the low achievement of its overall student population. Another 18 percent of schools failed to meet AYP due to the low achievement of two or more subgroups. This means that most schools that failed to meet AYP had substantial groups of students who were not being well served by their schools. Although AYP results may be an imperfect barometer of opportunities to learn, in a large number of cases they can indicate systemic issues that need to be addressed.

Based on the promising results at Greenfield Elementary School and others like it, we know that school turnaround can be achieved. It requires district support and good leadership to advocate for change, but most importantly, it requires a highly committed faculty to embrace change and challenge itself to work through the painful process of recovery. It can be done, and it must be done if our nation is to fulfill its promise. There are tens of thousands of schools that need educators like you to advocate for improved teaching and learning in order to forge a better future for the children and youth of this country.

FOLLOW-UP ACTIVITIES

1. You and a group of concerned faculty members may want to read the case study found in the first part of this chapter and consider the similarities and differences with your school. Is the general faculty aware of the school's current status relative to state and federal requirements? Is it satisfied with the status? What would it take to assist the

faculty in improving the school's status? What changes made at Greenfield Elementary School appeal to you and could be implemented in your setting?

2. Because each school has its own set of distinct circumstances and challenges, solutions must be crafted from a broad range of possibilities that are tailored to the context. It is often helpful to attend regional or national conferences to explore how other schools are addressing concerns and shaping new directions. Dialogue with other educators outside of your school and school district can bring new perspectives on your own situation.

ENDNOTES

1. Olson and Hoff 2006.

2. See discussion of this shift in professional development discussed by Linda Christensen in her article entitled, "Teacher Quality: Teachers Teaching Teachers" (Christensen 2005/2006).

3. See, for example, Duke 2004, Elmore 2005, and Fullan 2001.

4. For example, the Education Trust in Washington, D.C., and the Schott Foundation for Public Education in Cambridge, Massachusetts.

5. Data obtained from www.schoolmatters.com.

6. Olson and Hoff 2006.

7. Olson and Hoff 2006.

REFERENCES

Cawelti, G. 1999. *Portraits of Six Benchmark Schools: Diverse Approaches to Improving Student Achievement*. Arlington, VA: Educational Research Service.

Charles A. Dana Center. 1999. *Hope for Urban Education: A Study of Nine High-Performing, High-Poverty, Urban Elementary Schools*. Austin, TX: Charles A. Dana Center, University of Texas at Austin.

Christensen, L. 2005/2006. Teacher Quality: Teachers Teaching Teachers. *Rethinking Schools* 20(2). Retrieved February 14, 2007, from http://www.rethinking schools.org/archive/20_02/ttt202.shtml.

DuFour, R., R. Eaker, and R. DuFour, eds. 2005. *On Common Ground: The Power of Professional Learning Communities*. Bloomington, IN: National Educational Service.

Duke, D. L. 2004. *The Challenges of Educational Change*. Boston: Pearson.

Elmore, R. F. 2005. *School Reform from the Inside Out: Policy, Practice, and Performance*. Cambridge, MA: Harvard Education Press.

Fullan, M. 2001. *Leading in a Culture of Change*. San Francisco: Jossey-Bass.

Education Trust. 2006. The Education Trust Honors Five "Dispelling the Myth" Schools. October. Retrieved February 14, 2007, from http://www2.edtrust.org/EdTrust/Press+Room/DTM+Winners+2006.htm.

Illinois State Board of Education. 2001. *High Poverty–High Performance Schools*. Chicago: Illinois State Board of Education, Research Division, Assessment Division.

Izumi, L. T. 2002. *They Have Overcome: High-Poverty, High-Performing Schools in California*. San Francisco: Pacific Research Institute.

Kannapel, P. J., and S. K. Clements. 2005. *Inside the Black Box of High-Performing High-Poverty Schools*. Lexington, KY: Prichard Committee for Academic Excellence.

McGee, G. W. 2004. Closing the Achievement Gap: Lessons from Illinois' Golden Spike High-Poverty High-Performing Schools. *Journal of Education for Students Placed at Risk* 9(2): 97–125.

Olson, L., and D. J. Hoff. 2006. Framing the Debate. *Education Week*, December 13.

Reeves, D. B. 2003. *High Performance in High Poverty Schools: 90/90/90 and Beyond*. Englewood, CO: Center for Performance Assessment.

Schmoker, M. 2001. *The Results Fieldbook: Practical Strategies from Dramatically Improved Schools*. Alexandria, VA: Association for Supervision and Curriculum Development.

3

Why Are Some Schools Less Successful Than Other Schools?

There are not many questions concerning public education that have engendered more heated debate or preoccupied more researchers than the question that serves as the title of this chapter. Few schools, of course, are a total loss. Even low-performing schools register successes with some students. The problem is that too many other students fail to acquire the skills and knowledge necessary to move forward in life. We owe it to these young people to keep asking why some schools perform better than other schools.

This chapter looks at several offshoots of the title query. The first question concerns the origins of low school performance. Is it really necessary to know the reason why a school is low performing? Some people regard the quest for reasons or causes as an academic exercise of little practical value to educators. What good does it do, they suggest, to determine that low performance is rooted in factors beyond our control? Parents send their children to school, and teachers have to make the most of it, regardless of the conditions back home. Others contend that some causes of low performance are, in fact, subject to teachers' influence. Which brings us to the second focal question: Is there general agreement about the reasons for low school performance?

In this chapter we look at various explanations for low school performance. Some are associated with students, others with their parents, and still others with schools and those who work in them. There are even explanations of low school performance that derive from aspects of society itself. Our hope is that these efforts to explain why some schools are less successful than other schools will prompt individual reflection and group discussion. One consequence of such reflection and discussion may be a desire to learn more about the reasons for your own school's performance. Which brings us to a third important question: What can teachers do to increase their understanding of the reasons for their school's performance? This question will be addressed in chapter 4.

To illustrate the kind of insights that may result from exploring the origins of low school performance, we will share findings from a study of schools in the School Turnaround Specialist Program. These findings reveal the variety of school-based conditions that may be linked to low performance.

KEY QUESTIONS

1. Is it necessary to know the reasons why a school is low performing?
2. Is there general agreement about the reasons for low school performance?
3. What can teachers do to increase their understanding of the reasons for their own school's performance?

OUR DUTY TO DIAGNOSE

Is impatience a legitimate excuse for skipping diagnosis? Perhaps you have suffered certain physical symptoms, such as a sore throat. Since you lead a busy life and have precious little time to schedule a visit to your physician, you phone her office and ask the nurse to phone in a prescription for an antibiotic. When the nurse insists that you come in for an examination, you feel put out. Doesn't the nurse realize that you've had these symptoms before, and an antibiotic clears up the sore throat in a few days?

But what if your guess is incorrect? What if this time your sore throat is the first sign of esophageal cancer? An antibiotic is unlikely to do any good, and you will have wasted valuable time.

Teachers often feel that they know why students are not achieving to expected levels of performance. Your own professional judgment is of great value. But so, too, is your fellow teachers' judgment. And that of school administrators, parents, and students. No person's judgment is correct all the time. We must not allow our impatience to get about the business of teaching to prevent us from tracking down the possible causes of academic problems. The old adage about "two heads are better than one" holds true when it comes to diagnosing the origins of low school performance. The harm that can result from guessing incorrectly about why students are not doing well in school more than justifies the time spent searching for reasons.

> *Turnaround Trap:* The school turnaround process can be delayed or defeated by not carefully examining possible causes of low performance.

Imagine that one of your students is not doing well in your class. She seems unmotivated to learn and unresponsive to your efforts to help. If you never checked with your colleagues to see how she was doing in other classes, you might draw the conclusion that this student did not care about her education. By consulting other teachers, however, you can determine if her lack of interest is apparent elsewhere or only in your class. If she seems engaged in other classes, your efforts as a diagnostician must focus on determining what might be different about your class. Is it the particular collection of peers in your class? One peer in particular? Is it the subject matter? How you conduct your class? Your expectations? The clarity of your directions? Something you might have said or done that could have been misinterpreted? Discussing the student's performance with your colleagues and the student herself can yield valuable clues to her problems in your class.

Now imagine that your entire school is not performing well. The job of diagnosing the reasons, of course, becomes much more challenging than tracking down the causes of one student's difficulties. It certainly is not a job for one person. All educators in a low-performing school should regard it as their professional obligation to learn as much as possible about why many students are not doing as well as their peers in other schools. While some individuals may criticize such efforts as a "blame game" or a "witch hunt," the truth is that being a professional entails taking an interest in the causes of inadequate performance.

> *Turnaround Trap:* A fear of being blamed or blaming colleagues for low performance can prevent educators from figuring out why many students are struggling.

The importance of identifying as accurately as possible the causes of low performance is obvious. As the diagnosis goes, so goes the treatment. When politics, professional jealousy, and personal insecurity intrude on the diagnostic process, the result can be diagnoses that miss the mark and subsequent interventions that do little or no good. It also is important to realize that some individuals favor particular explanations for low school performance because they lead to "pet" cures. In other words, people may choose the intervention first and then search for a diagnosis that justifies the intervention. An example might be someone who is committed to small schools. To justify reducing school size, they focus only on causes that lead to this outcome, causes such as loss of student identity and the greater likelihood of serious discipline problems in large schools. By ignoring other possible causes, they run the risk of overlooking the needs of many students. We cannot afford to waste time, resources, and students' lives by conducting a careless or self-serving diagnosis of school problems.

Where can teachers look for help in their efforts to pinpoint the causes of low performance? Here's where we can be of assistance. We have explored the causes of low school performance in the schools participating in the School Turnaround Specialist Program. This process has involved listening to the experiences and insights of a number of teachers and principals.[1] In addition, we have combed recent research on low-performing schools and the achievement gap. As a result, we have identified a number of possible contributors to low school performance. These represent a starting place for your discussions and diagnostic efforts. One word of caution, however: In no case have we found that low school performance is traceable to a single factor or even a few factors. Do not be surprised if you discover a variety of contributors to low school performance. Schooling, after all, is a very complicated enterprise undertaken in a highly complex society.

> *Turnaround Tip:* Avoid the temptation to settle on a single simple explanation for low school performance. The likelihood is great that there are many contributing factors.

SEARCHING FOR SOURCES OF LOW SCHOOL PERFORMANCE

As you may have guessed, considerable debate and disagreement surround the causes of low school performance. Our goal in this section is not to take a position, but to provide an overview of various causes that have been identified in our own work and in the research of others. We begin with the fundamental element in every school—the student—and move on to other causal agents, including parents, peers, society in general, schools, and teachers.

Students

It strikes us as interesting that many explanations of low school performance appear to overlook the role of students. While it may be true that students are products of their cultures and their families, it would be a mistake to disregard the impact on student achievement of personality, motivation, self-esteem, and other personal characteristics over which young people exercise increasing influence as they grow older. Every teacher is aware that some students from impoverished backgrounds and broken families somehow manage to defy the odds and succeed in school. What causes these students to be so resilient while their peers spiral downward?

When Reginald Clark (1983) studied high-achieving and low-achieving African American twelfth graders from poor single-parent and two-parent families, he found that low-achievers still possessed surprisingly positive conceptions of themselves. Except where school success was concerned! These youngsters manifested a desire to improve themselves, but they did not see schooling as a means to that end.

John Ogbu (2003) was invited by African American parents in the affluent Cleveland suburb of Shaker Heights to study why many of their children, despite coming from well-to-do families headed by highly educated parents, lagged behind their White classmates. Ogbu's findings were similar to Clark's. African American students often failed to see how their present schooling contributed to their future as adult members of society. Even when they aspired to careers requiring academic preparation, such as engineering and medicine, they did not see a connection between pre-college coursework and eventual access to a career. Their failure to appreciate the relevance of academic work led to what Ogbu referred to as "academic disengagement." The signs of academic disengagement are well-known to all teachers: chronic absenteeism and tardiness, inattentiveness in class, and failure to turn in assignments.

Several years following Ogbu's study, another effort was made to understand the achievement gap in Shaker Heights (Ferguson 2001). Survey data were collected from virtually all seventh through eleventh graders in the school system. One conclusion of the survey was that a lack of skills more than a lack of effort accounted for the differences in achievement between African American and White students. African American students reported spending more time on homework than their White counterparts, but they also indicated a lower homework completion rate. The single largest predictor of the achievement gap turned out to be the proportion of courses taken at the honors and Advanced Placement levels. Ferguson did not speculate on the reasons for this difference in course-taking choices.

Interest in the noncognitive aspects of student success has grown in recent years, as evidenced by the success of Daniel Goleman's books on emotional intelligence (1996) and social intelligence (2006). This work finds that it is not just *what* students know that causes them to succeed or fail in school, but how they approach schoolwork and life in general (Tough 2006). One area of particular importance concerns self-discipline. Duckworth and Seligman (2006), for example, found that scores on a measure of self-discipline were more accurate predictors of grade point average than IQ scores, by a factor of two. Seligman (1991) long has maintained that students who are optimistic are more likely to do well in school than students who are pessimistic. The latter fail to see themselves as agents of their own improvement. When good things happen to them, they attribute these positive occurrences to factors other than their own effort and ability, but when misfortune befalls them, they assume responsibility.

Teachers on the lookout for ways that students contribute to their own lack of school success are advised to consider such characteristics as attitude toward school, aspirations, self-discipline, and pessimism. Other characteristics that can play a role in determining school success include adaptability, patience, openness, and willingness to ask for help. When students are unable or unwilling to adjust to different classroom environments, defer gratification, accept new ideas and advice, and solicit assistance when they do not understand something, the likelihood of doing well in school is dramatically reduced.

Parents

Those who believe that parents are responsible to a great extent for low school performance are aware of the various student-based factors noted in the preceding section, but they go on to point out that most students are not born with these characteristics. Their source, they insist, first must be sought at home. The environment in which children are raised exercises a powerful influence on their personality, beliefs, and behavior. Numerous studies have indicated that how parents communicate and interact with their children is closely related to the children's cognitive and emotional development. Many feel that much of a child's capacity for learning is determined before he enters kindergarten. For this reason, educators and policy makers often advocate expanding access to prekindergarten programs.

Problematic home environments are closely associated with poverty. When Betty Hart and Todd Risley (1995) studied forty-two families with newborn children, they found that vocabulary growth differed sharply by socioeconomic status. By age three, children of parents on welfare had roughly half the vocabulary of more well-to-do children. The average IQ of the poor children was seventy-nine, thirty-eight points lower than the better-off three-year-olds. Hart and Risley reported that the differences in parent communication patterns were closely tied to differences in their children's development. Poor parents had less to say to their children than well-to-do parents, and their comments were more likely to be "discouragements" and negative comments than "encouragements."

The impact of parents and home environments does not disappear as children grow older. When Clark (1983) compared the home life of high-achieving and low-achieving high school seniors, he discovered a number of differences. Some of these differences are listed below:

High Achievers	Low Achievers
Frequent school contact initiated by parent.	Infrequent school contact initiated by parent.
Parents psychologically and emotionally calm with child.	Parents in psychological and emotional upheaval with child.
Parents expect to play a major role in child's schooling.	Parents have lower expectations of playing role in child's schooling.
Parents expect child to get postsecondary schooling.	Parents have lower expectations that child will get postsecondary schooling.
Parents have explicit achievement-centered rules and norms.	Parents have less explicit achievement-centered rules and norms.
Conflict between family members is infrequent.	Conflict between family members is frequent.
Parents provide liberal nurturance and support.	Parents are less liberal with nurturance and support.

Clark's investigation reveals critical differences in parent expectations, interactions, and home operations. Ogbu's (2003) study of African American families in Shaker Heights suggests that differences in child-rearing may not be a function of socioeconomic status alone. Many parents, including those who were relatively affluent, lacked sufficient understanding of how grouping practices worked in middle and high school. As a result, they did not stress the importance of honors and advanced classes to their children.

Failure to understand the workings of the school system should not be assumed to result from low parental expectations. Ogbu's findings challenge Clark's in that the former researcher found that most Shaker Heights parents in his study, regardless of socioeconomic status, possessed high academic expectations for their children. When Ogbu's research team spoke with students, however, they learned that students felt that their parents did not show them how to succeed in school or closely supervise their schoolwork. Having high expectations and telling children that they need to do well in school, in other words, are no substitute for actually explaining how to get good grades.

Various factors can compound the impact of the preceding examples of parent contributions to low school performance. When divorce is added to the picture, parents may have less time and emotional energy to devote to their children's schooling. Single parents, especially when they must work outside the home, face enormous challenges trying to stay abreast of their children's schoolwork. When a parent does not speak English, the challenge can seem almost insurmountable. Understanding how a student's home life is contributing to their difficulties in school, of course, does not justify giving up on the student. Such information, however, should be used to develop a realistic plan of assistance for the student.

Peers

As children mature, their parents continue to be important influences, but the adolescent peer group also becomes a factor in shaping beliefs and behavior. Peers, of course, can exercise a positive or a negative influence when it comes to schoolwork. When their influence is negative, it often is associated with the so-called fear of success syndrome. The argument goes as follows: Young people learn to fear success because of its perceived social consequences. When girls in middle school go out of their way to avoid doing well in math and science, they may be doing so in order to escape being labeled as a "brain." Girls may perceive that being too smart is a disadvantage when it comes to meeting boys. A similar phenomenon has been linked to some male athletes in high school. These individuals feel that they must do well enough to maintain eligibility to play sports, but they fear being ridiculed by their teammates if they excel in school.

Ogbu (2003) detected negative peer influence in his study of academic disengagement among African American students in Shaker Heights. The origins of this negative influence can be traced, he argued, to the perception that the school curriculum had been imposed on Blacks by Whites. Doing well in school was derided by some African American students as "acting White." Behaviors associated with "acting White," according to Ogbu's research, include using standard English, enrolling in honors and Advanced Placement classes, acting "smart" during lessons, and hanging out with too many White students. Some African American students even expressed the belief that doing well in school risked the loss of one's Black identity.

Poverty

It is no mere coincidence that many, if not most, low-performing schools are located in poor neighborhoods and enroll large percentages of children from poor families. Poverty and low achievement long have kept each other company. We have already read about research on the relationship between poverty and parenting. Poor parents often confront a gauntlet of challenges just to provide food and shelter for their children. Their ability to participate in their children's schooling suffers as a result. Poor children also are more likely to live in settings that lack adequate places to study and access to technology and instructional materials. Mobility is another problem associated with poverty. Unable to pay rent, many poor families are constantly on the move (Rothstein 2004). When students continually switch from one school to another, they are less likely to do well in school. As poor children grow older, they may be compelled to find jobs in order to supplement family incomes. The need for employment limits the time available for homework and study and sometimes leads young people to drop out of school entirely.

Besides these direct effects of poverty on student achievement, school performance can be indirectly affected by inadequate school resources. Poor families tend to live in localities where property values are relatively low and viable commercial enterprises are scarce. The results are a diminished tax base and less revenue available to support public education. In one study conducted by the Education Trust (Wilkins 2006), school districts that served the greatest number of poor and minority students were found to consistently receive less state and local money than other school districts—roughly $614 less per pupil in 2003. Jonathan Kozol (1991) dramatized the huge gap between poor and well-to-do school systems in his disturbing book, *Savage Inequalities*. Kozol described the conditions in which students had to learn in poor districts like East St. Louis and San Antonio and in their wealthy suburban neighbors. Schools in the poor districts lacked up-to-date textbooks, computers, and even working heating and cooling systems. It is not hard to understand why students in the poor districts faced an uphill struggle when it came to learning and doing well in school.

These problems are compounded by the fact that schools in poor communities have difficulty competing for the most highly qualified teachers (Lankford, Loeb, and Wyckoff 2002). Talented young teachers that start out in poor schools frequently move on to "greener pastures" at the first opportunity. Teacher turnover in poor schools typically is higher than in other schools, resulting in lost expertise and diminished instructional continuity.

Society

How could a nation as blessed with resources and talent as the United States allow the students who are most dependent on the public schools to be exposed to the kinds of deplorable conditions described previously? To answer this question, it is necessary to examine the values and priorities of our society. Society invests in what it values. The greater the investment, the greater the perceived worth. Public school teachers need only compare their paychecks with those of other professionals to understand this point. The preceding section cited research indicating that school systems serving greater numbers of poor and minority students received less state and local money than other school systems. Such a differential allocation of resources is hardly an accident. Cities like Cleveland, Cincinnati, and Washington, D.C., can find hundreds of millions of dollars to build new stadiums while the facilities in which their young people go to school continue to deteriorate. Would a society that truly valued public education for less-advantaged children tolerate such negligence?

Opportunity structure is another area where society influences the schooling of poor children. Opportunity structure refers to the possibilities that await young people when they complete their education. Ogbu (2003) found that African American students from both well-to-do and less well-off families did not see a close connection between what they were expected to do in school and what was needed to succeed in the adult job market. The problem in some cases involved the perceived irrelevance of the school curriculum. In other instances, students doubted that their educational experiences could overcome the forces of job market discrimination, forces that they believed held back many adults that they knew.

One of the most insidious ways that poor children, especially poor minority children, can be adversely affected by mainstream society involves the process of "internalization." Ogbu (2003) explained that internalization occurs when members of a minority group consciously or unconsciously accept as accurate the assessment of their abilities and prospects held by the majority group. That internalization is more than a social science abstraction is revealed in the following poignant comment by a Black high school student who was interviewed by a member of Ogbu's research team: "Sometimes in the classroom, [Black] kids seem to think, to have this mentality, this unconscious way of thinking that Blacks are inferior to Whites. And I think that takes a toll on some Black students" (2003, 78).

Schools

Reading about the possible causes of low school performance up to this point may have been frustrating. Perhaps you are wondering, what can I do about inadequate parenting, poverty, and misguided social values? As an individual teacher or even a member of a faculty, you may not be able to tackle such pernicious and persistent problems on your own. Still, it is important to get these causes "on the table," if only to identify some of the reasons why educators in low-performing schools frequently feel helpless. Our purpose in writing this guide, however, is not to reinforce feelings of helplessness. We therefore need to reiterate one very important fact: There are many schools serving poor students in beleaguered communities that are performing well above expectations (*Dispelling the Myth* 1999; *Hope for Urban Education* 1999; *Wisconsin's High-Performing/High-Poverty Schools* 2000). We hope you got this message as you read the previous chapter. How have these schools been able to overcome the odds? The short answer is this—these schools focused on correcting what was in their power to correct rather than bemoaning problems that were beyond their control.

This observation brings us to an important and potentially painful realization. Some of the problems facing low-performing schools are of their own creation. Physicians long ago acknowledged that they contribute to many health problems. They even created a special branch of their profession—iatrogenic medicine—devoted to problems that arise *after* patients visit a hospital or see a physician. Education probably could use a comparable specialty. Students often experience problems that derive from how they are treated *in school*. These are the problems that we are most likely to be able to correct. But first we have to recognize them. It is not always easy to recognize what is going on right in front of us. Here is where we can offer some help. In this section we want to share some of the school-based contributors to low performance that we have identified in our research on school turnarounds (Duke 2006; Duke et al. 2005). We divide them into organizational, cultural, and instructional contributors.

Organizational Contributors

Schools are complex organizations located in school districts, which are also complex organizations. Organizational complexity refers to the fact that the mission of schools and school districts is multifaceted and the means for achieving the mission are varied and complicated. As you doubtless are aware, public schools must address the needs of gifted students, disabled students, non-English-speaking students, and students who have not been identified for special services. Students are expected to master a set of basic curriculum objectives, typically based on state standards, but they also are expected to acquire the knowledge necessary to gain access to postsecondary education or entry-level employment. Schools, in addition, are often charged with addressing various health and welfare needs of students. Faced with so many responsibilities, educators can lose a sense of focus and direction. Everything appears to be a high priority. And that creates a serious obstacle to school improvement. If everything is a high priority, nothing is a high priority. Schools do not have access to unlimited resources. When educators try to spread their time and energy across a broad set of goals, they often encounter problems. We have found that many low-performing schools lack a clearly articulated focus and a relatively narrow set of priorities that all agree should serve as the first order of business.

> *Turnaround Trap:* Treating every problem as a high priority reduces the likelihood that any particular problem will be resolved.

Lack of focus and direction are organizational problems frequently associated with inadequate leadership. School principals and teacher leaders are supposed to provide clarity regarding which concerns require immediate attention and which concerns can be deferred. Inadequate leadership is associated with most of the possible causes of low school performance addressed in this section. It is not uncommon, in fact, for new principals to be assigned to schools embarking on the turnaround process.

A principal cannot single-handedly turn around a school, however. Unfortunately, many low-performing schools are characterized by a lack of effective teamwork. While some of the problem may involve the particular makeup of teams and personality clashes between team members, lack of time to meet together during the school day also is an issue. Effective teams typically meet on a regular basis to do such things as plan lessons, analyze data on student progress, identify students who are struggling, and organize instructional interventions. When the school schedule provides little or no time for such collaboration, teams are less likely to function effectively.

In some low-performing schools that we have studied, teachers were not organized into teams at all. There were no grade-level teams to ensure coverage of curriculum standards, no vertical teams to articulate the curriculum across grade levels, no student assistance teams to coordinate the delivery of help to struggling students, no school improvement teams to identify targets for reform, and no leadership teams to monitor school-wide progress. The absence of organizational infrastructure meant that each teacher functioned more as an independent agent than as a member of a faculty committed to a common mission. Turning around a low-performing school is far too great an undertaking for individual teachers acting in an uncoordinated way.

Another organizational obstacle concerns the absence of data related to student achievement. It is not enough to wait until students take end-of-year tests. By that time it is too late to provide timely assistance. Teachers, of course, give students homework assignments, quizzes, and tests to determine how well they are doing. Sometimes, however, the variation between teacher assessments is considerable. We have found that teachers in low-performing schools do not always align their assessments with the curriculum standards on which end-of-year tests are based. There is no substitute, we believe, for regularly administered assessments of student progress—sometimes referred to as benchmark tests. Such assessments may be best arranged on a schoolwide rather than a teacher-by-teacher basis.

Low-performing schools are frequently characterized by certain policies and practices that can place many students at a disadvantage. The policy of tracking students into college-preparatory, vocational, and general tracks has been criticized as a form of institutional discrimination because poor and minority students are often underrepresented in the college-preparatory track. A similar indictment has been leveled at grouping practices that permanently separate high achievers and low achievers. Grouping practices that are effective provide low achievers with the skills and knowledge to move to higher-achieving groups. School suspension practices also have caused concern for student advocates. A disproportionate number of minority and low-achieving students are suspended from school every year. It goes without saying that students who are not in school are unlikely to learn what they need to learn.

A school is no better than its faculty. Teaching has always been a complex enterprise, but teaching today in a low-performing school presents an array of challenges that many would claim are unprecedented. Expectations for students, including those who in the past might have been allowed to get by with marginal performance, have never been higher. Policy makers and the public want schools to prepare young people to succeed in an increasingly competitive global economy. Under such circumstances, teachers must continually upgrade and fine-tune their pedagogical skills and curriculum knowledge. Staff development and in-service training in low-performing schools, unfortunately, is often unfocused, isolated, and irrelevant. Teachers receive "one-shot" workshops unrelated to the specific needs of their students and the instructional programs in place at their school. Long-term arrangements with outside consultants are rare. The entire faculty often is required to sit through training that is pertinent to only a few teachers.

> *Turnaround Tip:* Low-performing schools frequently are characterized by organizational problems, including
>
> • Lack of focus and direction
> • Ineffective or nonexistent teams
> • Schedules that do not provide adequate time for teamwork
> • Lack of timely data on student progress
> • Inadequate staff development

Cultural Contributors

Schools are characterized by cultures and subcultures. This is true even for low-performing schools. Cultures often serve as conservative forces preserving the status quo. Preserving the status quo in a high-performing school may be acceptable, but such is not the case in a low-performing school where change is desperately needed. It is hard to pinpoint the elements of a school culture, especially for the people within a school. The school culture is embodied in the values, beliefs, and assumptions that members of the school take for granted. Sometimes it takes a stranger or a newcomer to recognize the key elements of a school's culture.

Teachers in high-performing schools often believe that all students can learn. Guided by this belief, they expose all students, not just a select group, to challenging material. Teachers in low-performing schools may express the belief in public that all students can learn, but when they are observed in the classroom, their actions sometimes belie their words (Good and Brophy 2003). Students who are perceived to be less able academically are asked less-challenging questions, given less time to respond, and assigned easier classwork and homework. Students are very much aware of such differential treatment, as revealed in the following quote from Rhona Weinstein, an expert on the impact of teacher expectations: "[E]lementary school children, even young ones, know that teachers, on average, treat high and low achievers differently within the same classroom. High expectations, trust, and opportunity from teachers are linked with doing well in school, whereas scolding, monitoring, and lots of help are associated with poor performance" (2002, 110).

How teachers account for low student performance also may reveal important clues as to the nature of school culture. In many low-performing schools, blame for low performance may be directed elsewhere—inadequate resources, lack of parental support, negative peer influence, and the like. While these factors may, indeed, have an impact on student achievement, teachers must be willing to "own" part of the problem if the school is to stand any chance of being turned around. Teachers, after all, should not take credit for student success if they are unwilling to assume some responsibility for student failure. The belief that teachers can and do make a difference in student learning is the bedrock of a constructive school culture.

There are many indicators of school culture that need to be examined before mounting any substantial effort to improve teaching and learning. How do teachers feel about working collaboratively? Do most teachers prefer to plan alone? How do teachers feel about providing additional assistance to struggling students? Do teachers embrace a sink-or-swim philosophy where they expect struggling students to initiate efforts to obtain help? How do teachers view parents? Do teachers resent parents who question how their children are being taught? What about incentives and rewards? Do teachers believe in providing students with material encouragement? When rewards are distributed, are they given only to the top achievers? How do teachers think about staff development? Do they believe they have mastered all aspects of teaching or are they willing to acknowledge that instructional skills, assessment practices, and classroom management techniques can always be refined and improved? The answers to questions like these should offer important insights regarding school culture and whether or not it is a contributor to low performance.

Turnaround Tip: Low-performing schools often are characterized by distinctive values, beliefs, and assumptions about what students and teachers are capable of accomplishing.

Instructional Contributors

Many people acknowledge that the way out of low performance is paved with good instruction. It is therefore reasonable to assume that one possible cause of low performance is inadequate instruction. Such a consideration, however, can be a very sensitive matter for many teachers who feel they already are giving their all to help students be more academically successful.

When we studied conditions in low-performing schools participating in the School Turnaround Specialist Program at the University of Virginia, we found in many cases that classroom instruction was not carefully aligned with the curriculum standards on which state standardized tests were based. Depending on the teacher, students might or might not be exposed to essential content.

Another problem concerned instructional interventions for struggling students. Because data on student progress was not collected and analyzed systematically, students frequently failed to receive timely and targeted assistance. Tutoring and other forms of help might be available, but they were not linked closely to individual students' particular weaknesses. The effectiveness of programs to help students in academic difficulty was rarely evaluated. Some assistance programs continued to operate, despite plummeting test scores.

In certain cases, instructional problems can be traced to lack of teacher experience and inadequate training. Low-performing schools often are characterized by high percentages of new teachers and teachers who lack the proper credentials to handle their assignments. These individuals often have difficulty maintaining orderly classrooms where students can focus on learning. In other instances, veteran teachers complain about being "burned out" after years of trying to teach under daunting conditions. It is difficult for these teachers' students to get excited about learning because they can see that their teachers are uninspired. Low-performing schools frequently lack up-to-date technology and instructional materials to support effective teaching and learning.

Turnaround Tip: Low-performing schools often are characterized by ineffective instruction and inadequate assistance for struggling students.

AGREEMENT IS ELUSIVE

We have briefly noted some of the most frequently mentioned causes of low school performance. Other reasons certainly could be added, including challenging state and federal mandates, local policies that put certain groups of students at a disadvantage, lack of central office support, and intrusive political maneuverings. Given the variety of explanations for low school performance, it is hardly surprising that certain interest groups favor particular explanations. Those that oppose additional funds for public education, for example, often place blame on teacher preparation. Educators often are inclined to trace poor student achievement to lack of parental support and involvement. Others find fault with policy makers, politicians, and educational leaders. We are convinced, however, that no single explanation can account for the fact that some schools perform less well than other schools. In searching for reasons for low performance, you should be prepared to identify multiple contributors.

Diagnosing the causes of a particular school's problems may not be a straightforward matter of determining the presence or absence of certain elements. In our own research we have discovered that low-performing schools can be characterized by many of the same policies, programs, processes, and practices found in high-performing schools. The difference lies in how well these policies, programs, processes, and practices are implemented. Teams, for example, frequently are found in both high and low-performing schools. In the former, however, teams function as truly collaborative groups engaged in identifying student deficits and providing timely assistance. In low-performing schools, on the other hand, teams are more likely to engage in defensive actions designed to deflect responsibility for student achievement.

> *Turnaround Tip:* Just because a low-performing school has a desired element in place is no guarantee that this element is functioning effectively.

It goes without saying that getting to know your school requires a considerable amount of reflection and honesty. In the next chapter we take a look at various ways that teachers can enhance their understanding of their school and the factors that are holding down performance.

FOLLOW-UP ACTIVITIES

1. Because discussing the causes of low performance at your own school can be a threatening and anxiety-provoking way to begin the turnaround process, it may be useful to start by reading a book or article about other schools that faced the need to improve. You and your colleagues can share reactions to the reading and discuss its applicability to your own school. A particularly useful book is John U. Ogbu's *Black American Students in an Affluent Suburb*.

2. Another preliminary activity might be to arrange for a team of teachers from your school to visit a comparable school that already has begun to turn itself around. Members of the visiting team can inquire about what their hosts found were contributors to low school performance and how they chose to address them.

ENDNOTE

1. Among the dedicated educators who contributed their insights to this book are the following: Melva Belcher, Deloris Crews, Nancy Conor, Joyce Harrison-Coleman, Parker Land, Melissa Marshall, Iris Page, Harry Reasor, Sharon Richardson, Mel Rose, Wayne Scott, Rosalind Taylor, Catherine Thomas, and Kim Yates.

REFERENCES

Clark, Reginald M. 1983. *Family Life and School Achievement*. Chicago: University of Chicago Press.

Dispelling the Myth: High Poverty Schools Exceeding Expectations. 1999. Washington, DC: Education Trust.

Duckworth, Angela Lee, and Martin E. P. Seligman. 2006. Self-discipline Gives Girls the Edge: Gender in Self-discipline, Grades, and Achievement Test Scores. *Journal of Educational Psychology* 98(1): 198–208.

Duke, Daniel L. 2006. *Keys to Sustaining Successful School Turnarounds*. Charlottesville, VA: Partnership for Leaders in Education.

Duke, Daniel L., et al. 2005. *Lift-off: Launching the School Turnaround Process in Ten Virginia Schools*. Charlottesville, VA: Partnership for Leaders in Education.

Ferguson, Ronald F. 2001. A Diagnostic Analysis of Black-White GPA Dispari-
ties in Shaker Heights, Ohio. In Diane Ravitch, ed., *Brookings Papers on Educational Policy 2001*, 347–414. Washington, DC: Brookings Institution Press.

Goleman, Daniel. 1996. *Emotional Intelligence*. New York: Bantam.

———. 2006. *Social Intelligence*. New York: Bantam.

Good, Thomas L., and Jere E. Brophy. 2003. *Looking in Classrooms*. 9th ed. Boston:
Allyn and Bacon.

Hart, Betty, and Todd R. Risley. 1995. *Meaningful Differences in the Everyday
Experiences of Young American Children*. Baltimore, MD: P. H. Brookes.

*Hope for Urban Education: A Study of Nine High-Performing, High-Poverty, Ur-
ban Elementary Schools*. 1999. Austin: Charles A. Dana Center, University of
Texas.

Kozol, Jonathan. 1991. *Savage Inequalities*. New York: Crown.

Lankford, Hamilton, Susanna Loeb, and Wyckoff. 2002. Teacher Sorting and the
Plight of Urban Schools: A Descriptive Analysis. *Educational Evaluation and
Policy Analysis* 24(1): 37–62.

Ogbu, John U. 2003. *Black American Students in an Affluent Suburb*. Mahwah,
NJ: Erlbaum.

Rothstein, Richard. 2004. The Achievement Gap: A Broader Picture. *Educational
Leadership* 62(3): 40–43.

Seligman, Martin E. P. 1991. *Learned Optimism*. New York: Knopf.

Tough, Paul. 2006. What It Takes to Make a Student. *New York Times*, November 26.

Weinstein, Rhona S. 2002. *Reaching Higher*. Cambridge, MA: Harvard University
Press.

Wilkins, Amy. 2006. *Yes We Can*. Washington, DC: Education Trust.

Wisconsin's High-Performing/High-Poverty Schools. 2000. North Central Regional Educational Laboratory.

4

Inquiring into the Health of Your School

You get sick, you seek a diagnosis from someone trained to recognize medical problems. When a school "gets sick," the first step toward recovery should involve identifying the problem or problems and the possible causes. In examining various kinds of organizational turnarounds, Kanter (2004, 165) argues that an "important step is putting a name to problems that have long gone unexpressed." It goes without saying that if organization members are unable or unwilling to name certain problems holding back their organization, the organization is less likely to improve. Consider the impact of naming long-standing problems such as "child abuse" and "sexual harassment." These troubling behaviors have existed for thousands of years, but until they were named, politicians, policy makers, journalists, and members of the public lacked commonly understood terms by which to refer to them.

Teachers are excellent sources of information and insight regarding the origins of low school performance. The aspects of teaching that cause teachers concern and lead to feelings of frustration are likely to be closely related to at least some of the sources of low school performance. When the diagnostic process is done well, teachers become active participants in seeking explanations for student achievement problems. The diagnostic process, in fact, represents an excellent opportunity to kindle or rekindle a spirit of cooperation and collective inquiry among the faculty. When the British National Audit Office investigated efforts to improve poorly performing schools in England, they looked for keys to sustaining improved student achievement after initial school turnaround efforts. What they

47

found bears directly on the focus of this chapter. One of the most prominent features of schools that continued to improve was the presence of a culture of self-evaluation (*Improving Poorly Performing Schools in England* 2006, 50). Such a culture is characterized by the willingness of teachers and administrators to continuously examine school programs, student performance, and their own actions. There is no better way to move toward a culture of self-evaluation than to begin the school turnaround process by examining possible sources of low school performance.

In order for collective inquiry to be productive, of course, teachers and other participants must be willing, in the words of Jim Collins (2001), "to confront the brutal facts." Care must be taken to prevent the diagnostic process from degenerating into excuse making and blame shifting. You would not conceal vital information from your physician if you wanted an accurate diagnosis. The same is true when diagnosing school performance problems. The inquiry process should be conducted in ways that encourage and reward, rather than punish, honesty and openness. Setting ground rules in advance concerning how to handle sensitive and possibly self-incriminating information is critical to the success of the process.

> *Turnaround Trap:* Efforts to determine the causes of low performance can degenerate into excuse making and blame shifting.

The process of diagnosing the causes of a school's low performance entails several components. First, the specific nature of inadequate student achievement must be pinpointed. Are students, for example, performing poorly in all subjects and at all grade-levels or are problems limited to particular subjects and subgroups of students? Once student achievement problems have been specified, the diagnostic process can shift to identifying the likely causes of the problems. To repeat an earlier point, it is almost never the case that the etiology of achievement problems can be traced to a single cause. Educators should be prepared to identify multiple contributors to low performance. Once possible causes have been located, those involved in the diagnostic process are ready for the last phase — culling out the causes over which they exercise little or no control. It is important, of course, to raise public awareness of *all* the factors contributing to low school performance, but the school turnaround process, at least in its early stages, should concentrate on those causes that teachers and administrators can affect.

The first section of this chapter examines the process of determining the specific nature of student achievement problems. The following section investigates various sources of information that can be tapped in order to learn about the likely causes of these student achievement problems.

IN WHAT WAYS ARE STUDENTS STRUGGLING?

In order for a school to be considered low performing, student achievement must be well below a level considered to be necessary for students to progress through the grade levels, graduate, and take the next steps toward a meaningful adult life. Politicians and educators, of course, debate the exact nature of an adequate education. Still, it is painfully obvious when a school's level of student achievement is well below that of other schools. Educators in these schools know that their students will be at a disadvantage when competing for college admission and jobs. The first step in the diagnostic process therefore should involve identifying those areas of the curriculum where student achievement is judged to be inadequate. Once trouble spots have been found, it is necessary to determine whether most students or only certain students are struggling with the content. If only certain students are struggling, do the students share certain common characteristics?

A useful approach to analyzing student achievement involves focusing on standardized test scores over the past five years. Since the advent of the federal No Child Left Behind Act in 2002 and various state educational accountability mandates, students have been expected to take and pass standardized tests in reading and language arts, mathematics, and other subjects. Most students in grades three through eight are tested. High school students in many states are expected to take and pass certain end-of-course standardized tests. By examining student achievement over time, teachers can answer a variety of important questions, including those listed below.

DIAGNOSTIC QUESTIONS CONCERNING
STUDENT ACHIEVEMENT ON STANDARDIZED TESTS

- Is there a trend over time in student test scores in a particular subject?
- Is there a trend over time for student test scores at a particular grade level?

- Is there a point in time at which test scores dropped dramatically?
- When test data is disaggregated by student subgroup, do certain subgroups perform worse on certain tests than other subgroups?
- When test data is disaggregated by teacher, do certain teachers' students perform less well than other teachers' students? (It is also important to determine whether certain teachers are assigned larger numbers of low-achieving students.)
- Are test results reported in such a way that teachers can examine student achievement in specific elements of a subject? If so, do students perform better in certain elements of the curriculum than in others? Or are student mistakes randomly distributed across the various elements of a curriculum?

Standardized tests from sources external to a school, of course, are not the only evidence of student achievement available to teachers. Teachers conduct a variety of classroom assessments over the course of a school year. It is therefore important to determine how student achievement on class tests, quizzes, and assignments compares to student scores on standardized tests. If class instruction is closely aligned to the content of standardized tests, class grades should be good predictors of standardized test scores.

Of all the subjects that students study in school, reading and language arts are the most critical. The reason is obvious. Practically every subject that students are taught requires them to be able to read. Even mathematics entails reading when it comes to word problems and directions in math textbooks. When we researched the first twenty schools in the School Turnaround Specialist Program, we found that low reading scores characterized every single school. Interestingly, though, some schools had low reading scores for one grade level but not for others, while other schools had low reading scores across the board. The same was true for scores on standardized tests of mathematics, although only twelve of the twenty schools were characterized by low math scores.

The search for the possible causes of low student achievement in reading and other subjects is bound to be affected by what is found in the initial investigation of student achievement over a five-year period. If achievement is relatively low across the board, for instance, a wide net must be cast in order to locate causes. If student achievement problems are limited to certain grade levels, subjects, and/or student subgroups, the search for causes can be more focused. Whether you ultimately employ a wide-angle lens or a microscope, the first step in diagnosing low school performance always should entail an analysis of student achievement data.

Turnaround Tip: The first step in diagnosing the causes of low school performance should involve an analysis of data on student achievement.

SEEKING THE CAUSES OF STUDENT ACHIEVEMENT PROBLEMS

Before reviewing some of the sources of data on the causes of student achievement problems, it is important to consider several tips about organizational diagnosis in general. First, never rely on a single source of information. Many studies of low-performing schools rely solely on the perspective of the principal. While principals are likely to possess a broad understanding of the challenges facing their schools, their views alone are unlikely to provide a balanced picture of all aspects of a school's program. The input of teachers, teacher leaders, and specialists is absolutely essential. So, too, is information from students, parents, and school volunteers. When a relatively objective and nonpartisan perspective is deemed necessary, it also may be important to call on the services of one or more outside observers.

A second tip is to take careful note of areas of investigation where there is substantial disagreement among individuals and groups. Differences of opinion regarding possible causes of student achievement problems can reveal important clues concerning why more progress is not being made in improving school performance. Disagreement about the causes of student achievement problems, in other words, may be a cause in and of itself! It is difficult to make headway against low performance when stakeholders do not share a common understanding of why problems exist.

Tip number three concerns what people do not say. Too often inquiry concerning educational issues focuses exclusively on what stakeholders say to interviewers or write on surveys and questionnaires. These responses, however, may reflect only what is judged to be "safe" and "socially acceptable." Alternatively, the responses may reflect what is easily called to mind. Possible causes that are rarely if ever mentioned should not necessarily be ruled out. Observations of what goes on in a school can serve as a useful check on what people say goes on in a school. People also have blind spots. Sometimes we are not prepared to recognize when a particular cause is at work. Each of us is predisposed to "see" certain sources of problems and not others. If you hire a communication consultant to analyze your school's problems, for example, you shouldn't be surprised when he discovers that your school suffers from communication breakdowns. That is what he is trained to see! He may not be trained, on the other hand, to recognize problems in the delivery of instructional assistance to struggling readers.

The final tip concerns the importance of trying to differentiate between symptoms and causes. We can waste a lot of valuable time addressing symptoms, only to discover that we have failed to confront the real causes of low school performance. Take student misbehavior in class, for instance. We may decide that misbehavior is a problem that must be eliminated before progress can be made in student learning. But what if the misbehavior only occurs in certain classes and is a direct result of inadequate instruction? Students grow restless because they cannot understand what their teachers expect, they do not keep up with assignments because directions are vague, and they fail to grasp written materials because their reading skills are inadequate. Under such circumstances, misbehavior may be a symptom, not a cause, of low performance. Until instructional issues are addressed, misbehavior is unlikely to subside.

> *Turnaround Tips:* In order for the diagnostic process to be as productive as possible, it is necessary to (a) rely on multiple sources of data, (b) take careful note of areas of disagreement, (c) attend to what people do not say as well as what they do say, and (d) distinguish between symptoms and causes.

In this section, we review four types of data that can yield insights regarding low performance: (1) data on students, (2) data on instruction, (3) data on school organization, and (4) data on school culture.

Data on Students

Any inquiry into the sources of low school performance should include data on student demographics. A major reason why student achievement plummets in some schools is the difficulty teachers experience adjusting to new groups of students with different backgrounds and abilities. When researchers studied the origins of low test scores at Hambrick Middle School in Aldine, Texas, for example, they found that the characteristics of students attending Hambrick had changed in the early 1990s (Picucci et.al. 2002). As wealthier families moved away to the suburbs, the student body increasingly consisted of economically disadvantaged students. In 1993–1994, 63 percent of Hambrick students qualified for free or reduced-price lunch. The Hispanic enrollment for that year rose to 64 percent, and many of these students had limited proficiency in English. What is encouraging about Hambrick is that 1993–1994 was the low-water mark for student achievement on the Texas Assessment of Academic Skills tests. Thanks to a concerted effort to turn the middle school around by school leaders, teachers, and the community, the percentage of students passing the TAAS tests steadily rose, until by 2001 over 90 percent of students achieved passing scores. What is even more impressive is the fact that these dramatic gains—up to 40 percentage points in seven years— were achieved while the percentage of economically disadvantaged students climbed from 63 to 80 percent and the percentage of Hispanic students grew from 64 to 72 percent.

The student population of a school can change in a variety of ways. The percentage of high-achieving students drops because a new magnet school opens. The percentage of economically disadvantaged students grows because of redistricting. A shift in school district policy results in the clustering of students with particular disabilities at a school. A government decision to send refugees to a particular region causes the overnight growth of a school's non-English-speaking population. Such demographic changes can strain a school's resources and challenge teachers' expertise.

Another source of student data offering insight into low school performance is attendance figures. When students miss school, they are more likely to fall behind their classmates. When students are chronically absent, they may never catch up. When analyzing attendance data, it is important to understand why students miss school. This may require reviewing written excuses and talking to students and parents. Absenteeism occurs for a variety of reasons, ranging from illness to school phobia and from boredom to child-care responsibilities. Knowing why students miss school is important when it comes to developing initiatives to improve attendance.

Another type of data on students that most schools routinely collect involves disciplinary problems. Some schools have sophisticated data management systems that record student violations of school and class rules and how the infractions are handled. Other schools simply have a stack of teacher referrals in the school office. Depending on the situation, student misconduct can be an indication of boredom, resentment, frustration at not understanding what is being taught, preoccupation with nonacademic concerns, or dislike of a teacher. An inquiry into the causes of low school performance should determine whether there are patterns to student misconduct. Do students, for example, misbehave more in certain classes than in others? Does their misbehavior tend to occur during certain times of the day? Are particular consequences for misconduct more effective than others? Is student misconduct related to academic difficulties?

Some data *about* students should be data *from* students themselves. One of us conducted a study of students in five middle schools (Duke 2001). Students were chosen because they were in academic difficulty but were not receiving special education services. Each student was asked to identify the reason or reasons why they were struggling with their coursework. They identified thirty-one different reasons, including the following:

- Does not complete assignments
- Performs poorly on tests and/or quizzes
- Does not pay attention in class
- Frequently is absent or tardy
- Is not liked by teacher
- Dislikes teacher or school
- Is bored with subject and/or school in general
- Does not participate in class activities
- Has difficulty with peers
- Lacks support at home
- Does not study for tests or quizzes
- Comes to class unprepared
- Disrupts class
- Experiences stress at home
- Does not manage time well

Students were brutally honest in their assessments of why they were not doing well in school. They rarely blamed others for their problems. Each student's guidance counselor and one of his or her teachers also were asked to identify the reason or reasons why they thought the student was experiencing academic problems. In some cases their answers corresponded to those given by the students, but in many instances they gave different answers. Determining why students and their teachers and counselors offer different explanations for low performance can be a useful focus for inquiry.

Students in the middle-school study also were asked a follow-up question. What did they think could be done to improve their schoolwork? The students identified fifty-nine different corrective actions, including the following:

- Student needs to pay better attention in class
- Parent(s) needs to check homework
- Student needs to complete homework before playing or watching television
- Student needs to write down all assignments
- Student needs to complete assignments on time
- Teacher needs to be more encouraging and caring
- Student needs to improve attendance
- Parent(s) needs to stress value of doing well
- Student needs to ask teacher for help when confused
- Student needs to keep track of how well s/he is doing in class
- Teacher needs to tell student what is expected of him
- Teacher needs to initiate assistance in class more often

Once again students gave candid responses that revealed their willingness to "own" their problems. In most cases they acknowledged that any improvement in their academic performance depended on their own initiative. Gathering information from students in low-performing schools has the potential to make them partners in the process of school improvement. At the very least, their responses to questions like those asked in the above middle-school study can serve as a basis for planning instructional interventions.

A great source of ideas about how to gather informative data from students is the book *Listening to Urban Kids* (Wilson and Corbett 2001). The book describes a study in which researchers spoke about school with 247 sixth-grade students enrolled in urban schools. The students were interviewed again a year later and the year after that. Students are in a unique position, the researchers point out, to compare classroom environments, teachers, and schools. In describing what they learned by listening to students, Wilson and Corbett wrote: "Students were very clear about what they wanted teachers to be like. . . . They wanted to spend their classroom time in the company of adults who were eager to help students without playing favorites, who were strict but nice and respectful, and who took the time to explain work clearly without becoming tediously repetitive" (32).

Another source of student input is class evaluations. Many teachers voluntarily ask students to evaluate their classes at the end of the year. Sometimes teachers employ standard checklists and rating forms, while others use clever assignments to gather evaluative data. One such assignment involves asking students to write a one-page letter to incoming students advising them on how to do well in the class. Such letters often reveal subtleties related to instructional routines, grading practices, and expectations of which teachers were unaware.

If you choose to distribute class evaluation forms to students, be certain to ask for information in ways that make sense to students. For years, teachers in the Milpitas Unified School District in California used an evaluation form that included a variety of items written so that students could easily understand them (Duke 1987, 118). Some of the items that students were asked to rate included the following:

- This teacher avoids treating certain students as favorites.
- This teacher explains lessons clearly.
- This teacher uses different ways and aids to help me learn.
- This teacher listens and tries to understand what we're saying.

We as adults always must remember that students have a unique perspective on what goes on in schools and classrooms, a perspective that is invaluable in trying to understand the sources of low school performance. Just because directions for an assignment are clear to an adult observer is no guarantee that all students grasp the directions. A teacher may feel that she encourages students to ask for help, but struggling students may see things differently. Valuing the voices of our students is a crucial component of the school turnaround process.

Data on Instruction

Some of the data from students mentioned in the previous section are related to instruction, but students are not experts on effective instructional practice in general. They, of course, can offer important clues about what does and does not work for them, but a full understanding of low school performance requires a more in-depth examination of instruction. Teachers, on the other hand, are able to offer important insights into how they plan, teach, assess, and handle classroom management. When researcher Mary Kennedy (2005, 159) interviewed teachers, she found that many were open to acknowledging aspects of instructional practice where they needed improvement. Among their targets of self-criticism were doing a better job of defining learning outcomes, fostering student learning, maintaining lesson momentum, fostering student willingness to participate, and establishing the classroom as a community. Actual observations of instruction by trained observers provide additional opportunities to identify teachers' classroom routines and determine how teachers deal with struggling students. The results of teacher reflections and classroom observations can be compared to research-based "best practices" in order to discover ways to improve instruction.

One way to examine instruction from a unique perspective is to shadow a student experiencing academic difficulties. When Dick Sagor was principal of West Linn High School in Oregon, he hired substitutes in order to free up twenty of his teachers to shadow twenty lower-track students for an entire day. Teachers began the day by explaining to students what they were doing and why. They sat next to their students in each class as well as lunch. They took notes on what they saw going on in class and how students responded. When the school day ended, teachers used their notes to debrief with the students. The teacher-observers learned that lower-track students frequently spent an entire class passively completing worksheets. There was very little active engagement in lessons. Being bored themselves, the teacher-observers came to understand why students in lower-track classes frequently "tune-out." The shadowing experience provided impetus for an initiative at West Linn High School to improve the quality of instruction in lower-track classes.

Another method for examining instruction that is similar to shadowing involves focusing on how one teacher works with one struggling student over the course of a semester or two. Similar to a clinical case study in medicine, this approach requires periodically meeting with a teacher to discuss how the student is doing and what efforts are being made to assist the student. Typically, the focus of classroom observations by peers and principals is the entire class. While it is important, of course, to understand how teachers deal with large groups, it is equally important to understand how teachers address the needs of individual students, particularly those experiencing academic difficulties. One study examined 229 elementary and secondary teachers and their work with particular struggling students over the course of a school year. It found that a student's best chance of getting individual assistance occurred between the beginning of the school year and the end of the first grading period (Duke and Gansneder 1998). The likelihood of students receiving individual assistance after the first grading period decreased dramatically! One possible explanation for this disturbing finding is that teachers tended to give up on students if their efforts to help during the first weeks of school failed to yield results.

Any inquiry into the origins of low school performance should also focus on the instructional interventions available to students in academic difficulty. There are three basic types of intervention: (a) interventions provided by the student's teacher during the regular school day, (b) interventions during the regular school day provided by someone other than the student's teacher, and (c) interventions provided outside of the regular school day. Since no single type of intervention is likely to be effective for all struggling students, it is important for schools to provide a variety of interventions and to monitor them closely to determine which interventions are working well and which are not. Interventions that are not producing the desired effects should be terminated in order to conserve resources.

When looking at what teachers do to help students master required material, it is important to determine whether they stick with interventions that are not working or whether they keep trying different interventions until they find ones that are effective. Table 4.1 provides an indication of the variety of possible interventions at a teacher's disposal. Drawn from teachers participating in the previously mentioned study of elementary and secondary teachers, the items in table 4.1 can be clustered into twelve relatively distinct types of intervention (Duke and Gansneder 1998). Using the interventions in table 4.1 as a starting place, you and your colleagues can investigate the extent to which students in academic difficulty receive particular types of assistance.[1] Be sure to add interventions that you know of that are not included in table 4.1.

Table 4.1. Inventory of Interventions for At-Risk Students

1.0 Adjustment of Expectations
- 1.1 Reducing requirements or expectations
- 1.2 Giving student "second chances" to complete work
- 1.3 Returning unacceptable work without a grade and asking student to redo it
- 1.4 Allowing student to retake tests and quizzes
- 1.5 Assigning student to a different ability group in class
- 1.6 Permitting student to be examined in an alternative mode

2.0 Adjustment of Instruction
- 2.1 Placing student in a self-pacing or "mastery" format, allowing more time to complete work
- 2.2 Utilizing special materials appropriate to student's ability level
- 2.3 Utilizing special materials of interest to the student
- 2.4 Assigning special homework
- 2.5 Providing opportunities for more practice (in terms of assignments and activities)
- 2.6 Providing opportunities to take practice quizzes and tests
- 2.7 Breaking down complex tasks/assignments into simpler, more easy-to-handle units
- 2.8 Modeling desired performance
- 2.9 Providing additional "structure" such as sequencing work in a logical, easy-to-follow order
- 2.10 Preteaching or reviewing vocabulary prior to lesson
- 2.11 Providing "hands on" assignments
- 2.12 Reading aloud to student
- 2.13 Listening to student read
- 2.14 Providing opportunities for independent study

3.0 Instruction in Supplementary Content
- 3.1 Study Skills
- 3.2 Problem solving and metacognitive strategies
- 3.3 Social Skills
- 3.4 Self-monitoring skills
- 3.5 Content related to self-esteem

4.0 Teacher-Initiated Counseling and Advisement
- 4.1 To diagnose problems and concerns
- 4.2 To explain expectations
- 4.3 To review assignments, tests
- 4.4 To brainstorm ideas for resolving problems
- 4.5 To apprise student of seriousness of situation
- 4.6 To review grades or progress

5.0 Tutoring or Reteaching by Teacher
- 5.1 During class
- 5.2 During regular school hours, but outside of class
- 5.3 Before or after school

6.0 Supervision and Monitoring
- 6.1 Reminders, friendly nagging
- 6.2 Close supervision during class
- 6.3 Assignment sheets
- 6.4 Student contract
- 6.5 Removing distractions, changing student's seat
- 6.6 Repeating/clarifying directions and instructions
- 6.7 Regular review of assignments, notebooks, etc.
- 6.8 Calling on student regularly during class

(continued)

Table 4.1. *(continued)*

7.0	Encouragement	10.0	Instructional Assistance in Class
7.1	Positive verbal reinforcement	10.1	Tutoring by teacher aid
7.2	Other forms of recognition (i.e. written, tangible rewards, etc.)	10.2	Tutoring by adult volunteer
		10.3	Peer tutoring
7.3	Behavior modification protocol	10.4	Cooperative learning instructional format
7.4	Grade "bargaining"	10.5	Consulting teacher
7.5	Opportunities for extra credit	11.0	Parent Communication and Involvement
7.6	Extra attention and caring	11.1	Home instruction or tutoring
7.7	Assigning extra responsibilities as a form of recognition (peer tutoring for example)	11.2	Parental monitoring at home (homework review, signed assignment sheets, etc.)
7.8	Focusing on what a student does well	11.3	Parental monitoring at school
7.9	Providing numerous opportunities for success	11.4	Progress reports to parents
8.0	Discipline	11.5	Parent-teacher conferences
8.1	Time-out or isolation (also can be used as a reward)	11.6	Parent-teacher phone calls
8.2	Lowering student's grade	11.7	Parent-teacher notes
8.3	Detention during school (recess, lunch)	11.8	Contact with a nonparent or "significant other" (sibling, grandparent, employer, minister, etc.)
8.4	Detention after school, Saturdays, etc.	12.0	Referral and Fact Finding
8.5	Loss of privileges	12.1	Roundtable or team meeting
8.6	Ignoring, withholding attention	12.2	Child study
8.7	Testing students on rules/consequences	12.3	Psychological assessment
9.0	Technology	12.4	School psychologist
9.1	Use of computer for remediation	12.5	School counselor
9.2	Use of computer as incentive	12.6	Private psychologist or counselor
9.3	Use of computer to develop cognitive ability	12.7	Pediatrician or other physician
9.4	Tapes of lessons (for follow-up, reinforcement, review of missed lessons)	12.8	Chapter 1
9.5	Tapes of lessons (for parent review, self-as-model intervention)	12.9	Resource room
9.6	Requiring student to make tape as part of assignment	12.10	Private tutor or learning center
		12.11	Study hall

12.12	Reading or math lab
12.13	Cross-age tutor
12.14	ESL
12.15	Special summer-school program
12.16	Afterschool program
12.17	Peer group or activity
12.18	Public agency
12.19	Reassignment to another teacher
12.20	School administrator
12.21	School social worker

In our study of schools in the School Turnaround Specialist Program, we found that they all had offered various instructional interventions prior to beginning the school turnaround process (Duke et. al. 2005). Just having instructional interventions, in other words, was not sufficient to raise school performance. The interventions have to be (a) based on actual data regarding student difficulties, (b) delivered in a timely manner, and (c) conducted by teachers with expertise in assisting struggling students. Once you and your colleagues have completed an inventory of the various instructional interventions available to students, you should make an effort to assess the effectiveness of each.

Since much of the initial instruction to which students are exposed takes place in groups, data also are needed on the quality of group instruction. Of particular importance is the alignment of instruction with the curriculum standards on which students are tested. These standards usually are derived from state and school district sources. It goes without saying that students who are not exposed to content on which they eventually will be tested are less likely to pass the standardized tests on which judgments of school performance are based.

Classroom assessment is another focus for investigation. As Richard Stiggins (2002) has observed, teachers should employ assessment to promote learning. Assessment *for* learning, not just assessment *of* learning, is how he puts it. To what extent do teachers in your school conduct frequent assessments of student progress? Do they analyze these assessments in order to determine areas of the curriculum where students need to be retaught? Are students encouraged to track their own performance? Are parents kept apprised of their child's progress?

A third component of good instruction is classroom management. Teachers in low-performing schools sometimes have difficulty managing their classrooms. Routines for handling various activities, including checking homework, distributing materials, and maintaining order, are sometimes missing. Teaching and learning in a disorderly classroom is a great challenge, sometimes *too great* for certain students. Research on effective classroom management has found that teachers need to develop a short list of essential rules and make certain that all students understand these rules (Good and Brophy 2003). Furthermore, teachers need to handle rule-breaking quickly, but without humiliating misbehaving students or disrupting instruction. Sound discipline is important, but it is never a substitute for a caring learning environment and positive teacher-student relationships.

Data on School Organization

How a school is organized can have a major impact on virtually everything that goes on in classrooms, from planning to instruction to interventions for struggling students. It is therefore crucial that any inquiry regarding the sources of low school performance include data on school organization. When investigating school organization, the central question to be answered is this: To what extent do aspects of the school's organization inhibit effective teaching and learning? Some of the "key aspects" were discussed in the previous chapter. They included organizational focus and priorities, teams and decision-making bodies, the school schedule, schoolwide provisions for monitoring student progress, and opportunities for ongoing staff development.

Teachers are a primary source of information regarding these and other aspects of school organization. Drawing on surveys, interviews, and focus groups, those charged with diagnosing school problems can learn whether teachers perceive that the school has a clear focus on learning and how teachers feel about elements of school infrastructure. Teachers should be asked to comment on the school schedule and the extent to which they have adequate time to reteach material on which students are struggling. Teacher input also is essential for determining a school's ability to pinpoint student academic problems in a timely manner and for evaluating the quality and relevance of staff development offerings.

Because they are uniquely prepared to see the overall picture, school administrators also should participate in the diagnostic process. They can help to identify variations across grade levels, subjects, and individual teachers. Such variations may reveal issues with articulation of the curriculum, coordination of instructional interventions, and implementation of school programs and policies. School administrators are an invaluable source of data regarding the adequacy of resources available to the school and the effectiveness of central office support.

Another component of the diagnostic process involves the review of documents in a school's archives. Previous accreditation reports and external reviews provide valuable information on how long certain problems have affected a school. Program evaluations and reports required by federal and state programs help in assessing the effectiveness of schoolwide interventions to assist students. The minutes of teacher teams and other school groups reveal persistent issues and how they were handled in the past.

As with other types of diagnostic data, investigators should take note of trends and discrepancies. Trends reflect problems and patterns of behavior that have persisted over time and which therefore merit close attention. Discrepancies represent areas where stakeholders disagree or see things differently. An effective diagnostic process seeks to understand why such discrepancies exist. It is difficult to turn around a school when stakeholders do not share a common perspective on the sources of low school performance.

Data on School Culture

School culture was described in the last chapter as the values, beliefs, and assumptions that school employees take for granted about a school. These values, beliefs, and assumptions influence how members of a school community think and act. Organizational culture often is regarded as "the way we do things around here." Perhaps you've visited other schools and noticed, almost from the moment you arrive, that these schools "feel" different from your school. The difference you detect may be traced in large part to variations in school culture. In chapter 3, we noted that it sometimes takes a stranger to recognize key aspects of a school's culture. This is due to the fact that it is hard for members of a school to recognize what they take for granted. Another way to appreciate aspects of a school's culture is to spend time in other schools. While schools share many common characteristics, they also embody certain unique qualities.

> *Turnaround Trap:* Asking members of a school to describe their school's culture is not always a productive exercise.

In order to learn more about your school's culture and the ways it may be contributing to low performance, a variety of strategies and queries can be employed. Your colleagues can be asked, for example, to relate a "success story" about the school. If people struggle to come up with a success story, if few of their stories are recent, or if their stories are unrelated to academic achievement, it may be that members of the faculty assume that nothing is working very well academically. Such responses are indicative of a school and a culture in decline.

Another probe involves asking individuals whom they consider to be a role model at the school and why. If the reasons why they regard certain colleagues as role models have little to do with pedagogical expertise or success in working with students, the school culture may stress the importance of other things, such as toughness concerning student discipline, success in athletics and extracurricular activities, and being well-liked by everyone. Turning around a low-performing school, however, may depend on the presence of pedagogically gifted role models and the valuing of instructional skill.

Asking people what they would like to preserve about their school if they embark on a course of major reform is one way to access feelings about a school culture's "core" values. If many people want to preserve the same elements of a school, these elements can be assumed to represent or symbolize core values. The elements may include a special program, a unique teaching arrangement, or a cherished ritual. If responses reveal few commonalities, the school culture may not be particularly robust.

In some schools, it is difficult to identify a single overarching culture. These schools may best be characterized as consisting of a collection of subcultures. Some high schools, for instance, consist of strong academic departments. The math department has its unique culture. So, too, do the social studies department and the performing arts department. The presence of strong subcultures can present an obstacle for those desiring to forge a common commitment to the school turnaround process.

How school members spend their time and how school resources are allocated provide additional insights regarding school culture. If teachers spend more time in team meetings bemoaning the home life of struggling students than thinking about what they can do to help these students, it could indicate a pervasive sense of hopelessness. If athletic coaches receive more attention and greater stipends than academic coaches, it may reveal ambiguity regarding the primary mission of the school.

Students, of course, offer important insights into a school's culture, especially if they have spent time in other schools (which is often the case, given the mobility rates of students in low-performing schools). Maehr and Midgley (1996, 221–25) helped to develop the Patterns of Adaptive

Learning Survey, a very useful tool for discovering how students characterize the culture of their school. The survey solicits student reactions to various statements, such as the following:

- Our teacher thinks mistakes are okay as long as we are learning.
- Our teacher wants us to understand our work, not just memorize it.
- Our teacher tells us how we compare to other students.

In order to investigate your school's culture, you can rely on ready-made surveys and questionnaires or develop your own. It is probably a good idea to enlist the assistance of a trained observer of school culture if you choose to develop your own data-gathering tool. Outside observers also may be helpful in recognizing important aspects of school culture.

Making Sense of the Data

Compiling data probably will seem easy compared to the job of analyzing and interpreting it and deciding what steps to take next. There are no quick and easy ways to make sense of the data on a low-performing school. What is crucial to the ultimate success of the school turnaround process is that the data are shared with stakeholders. While time-consuming, keeping stakeholders "in the loop" increases the likelihood they will support improvement initiatives. The entire process must be honest and "transparent." There is nothing to be gained from pretending that things are better than they are. Parents and community members know when a school is struggling. Educators must level with them if they expect to enlist their help. We often talk about children's "readiness" for school. It is important to bear in mind, however, that when you are diagnosing the causes of low school performance, you are trying to determine a school's "readiness" for children.

We close with an observation from our work on school turnaround projects. We have observed schools in which the task of diagnosing the causes of low performance was undertaken primarily by the principal and a few associates, and we have studied schools in which this work was a collaborative venture involving both administrators and faculty members. In our estimation, the latter have been more successful than the former, especially when faculty members were able to avoid getting defensive and were willing to take an open and honest look at their school.

FOLLOW-UP ACTIVITIES

1. Working either alone or with a few colleagues, develop a set of questions that you could ask your low-achieving students in order to better understand why they are having difficulty. Practice using the questions with a few students to see if their answers address issues over which you and your colleagues have some control. (If you believe that your own students may not give you honest answers, try using the questions with another teacher's students.)

2. Review several sets of your students' tests, quizzes, and/or assignments. Make a list of the mistakes that you noted when you graded the work. Do you see patterns in the mistakes (a) for individual students, (b) subgroups, and (c) for the class as a whole? Are mistakes randomly distributed? Based on your findings, what could be done to ensure that students do not repeat their mistakes?

3. Identify ten students who have "defied the odds" and done well in your school. Interview each student and find out how they account for their academic success and what school-based factors were important to them. Draw on this information to develop a set of intervention strategies for low-achieving students.

4. Use the list of instructional interventions in table 4.1 as a basis for discussions with your colleagues. Which of the listed interventions have they found to be effective? What additional interventions can they offer?

ENDNOTE

1. It is important to point out that the various interventions in table 4.1 do not necessarily represent "best practice." The interventions simply reflect what 229 teachers indicated that they did to assist struggling students.

REFERENCES

Collins, Jim. 2001. *Good to Great.* New York: Harper Collins.
Duke, Daniel L. 2001. *A Report on the Middle Schools of Albemarle County.* Charlottesville, VA: Thomas Jefferson Center for Educational Design.

Duke, Daniel, L. 1987. *School Leadership and Instructional Improvement*. New York: Random House.

Duke, Daniel L., and Bruce Gansneder. 1998. Staff Development Planning: Teacher Responses to the Needs of At-Risk Students. In Regis Bernhardt, Carolyn N. Hedley, Gerald Cattaro, and Vasilios Svolopoulos, eds., *Curriculum Leadership*, 89–106. Cresskill, NJ: Hampton.

Duke, Daniel L., et. al. 2005. *Lift-off: Launching the School Turnaround Process in Virginia Schools*. Charlottesville, VA: Partnership for Leaders in Education, University of Virginia.

Good, Thomas, and Jere Brophy. 2003. *Looking in Classrooms*. 9th ed. Boston: Allyn and Bacon.

Improving Poorly Performing Schools in England. 2006. London: National Audit Office, Department for Education and Skills.

Kanter, Rosabeth Moss. 2004. *Confidence*. New York: Crown Business.

Kennedy, Mary M. 2005. *Inside Teaching*. Cambridge, MA: Harvard University Press.

Maehr, M. L., and C. Midgley. 1996. *Transforming School Cultures*. Boulder, CO: Westview Press.

Picucci, A. C., Amanda Brownson, Rahel Kahlert, and Andrew Sobel. 2002. *Driven to Succeed: High-Performing, High-Poverty, Turnaround Middle Schools*. Austin: Charles A. Dana Center, University of Texas.

Stiggins, Richard J. 2002. Assessment Crisis! The Absence of Assessment *for* Learning. *Phi Delta Kappan* 83(10): 758–65.

Wilson, Bruce L., and H. Dickson Corbett. 2001. *Listening to Urban Kids*. Albany: State University of New York Press.

5

Planning: The First Step to Better School Performance

No school starts the turnaround process completely from scratch. Teachers and administrators doubtless have already tried a variety of strategies and interventions in the hopes of boosting student achievement. Whatever has been tried, unfortunately, has not worked well, at least for a number of students. In the preceding chapter we explored ways to gather data on the possible causes of continuing academic problems. These diagnostic activities are a key element in the planning of a school turnaround initiative. In this chapter we examine other key elements of planning. These include assessing a school's capacity for change, focusing on a manageable set of priorities, determining teachers' readiness for reform, and deciding whether to adopt, adapt, or create a program of change.

Sometimes a low-performing school enjoys the luxury of taking a year or more to plan a course of action leading to improved student achievement. In other cases, teachers and administrators must squeeze planning into a summer. And on occasion, educators are compelled to build the bridge while crossing it. Whichever the case, we recommend that the issues in this chapter be given serious consideration.

Planning, of course, must eventually give way to action. Chapter 6 is devoted to the actions that have been taken during the early months of the turnaround process in public elementary and secondary schools that have succeeded in raising student achievement. The advice in the present chapter as well as the one to follow draws on our own studies of schools in the University of Virginia's School Turnaround Specialist Program (Duke et. al. 2005) as well as four collections of case studies of school success (Johnson and Asera 1999; *Opening Doors* 2001; Picucci et. al. 2002; and *The Power to Change* 2005). No two school success stories with which we are familiar involve exactly the same "characters" and "plot." By sharing aspects of the planning process that have proven to be useful "first steps" in various low-performing schools, we hope to provide you and your colleagues with an idea of the decisions that will be needed in order to get the turnaround process "off the ground."

PROGRESS REQUIRES CAREFUL PLANNING

Low-performing schools exist in a world characterized by impatience. Parents are impatient about improving the quality of their children's schooling. Local businesses are impatient for schools to produce more capable graduates. Politicians are impatient about raising student achievement to a level that is competitive with other developed nations. Impatience, while clearly understandable, is the enemy of careful planning. Careful planning for school turnarounds should address four "core" questions, beginning with "What is the school's capacity for change?"

What Is the School's Capacity for Change?

"Capacity for change" can be a vague concept encompassing just about everything about a school. To narrow the focus without sacrificing thoroughness, Duke (2004, 132) has synthesized various ideas regarding capacity for change into three key elements: (a) a facilitative organizational structure, (b) an organizational culture that supports change, and (c) adequate resources to initiate and nurture change. Chapter 3, of course, noted that one or more of these elements may be missing in a low-performing school. The challenge of school turnaround is especially difficult when all three elements are missing. Let us consider each of these elements in greater detail.

> *Turnaround Tip:* Planning a school turnaround initiative should involve assessing the school's capacity for change.

Organizational Structure

In order for a school's "structure" to be considered "facilitative," arrangements should be in place to allow teachers and administrators to plan collaboratively, monitor progress, and develop corrective strategies on a continuing basis. These arrangements often include "horizontal" teams consisting of all faculty members working with students at a certain grade level and "vertical" teams consisting of faculty members from different grade levels. Horizontal teams in elementary schools frequently focus on comparing lesson plans to make certain that all students, regardless of their teacher, are exposed to essential content. In secondary schools, horizontal teams can consist of teachers from different subject matter areas working with the same group of students. When they meet, the focus may be curriculum coordination, staff development needs, or discussing students who are struggling academically.

Vertical teams typically are concerned with curriculum articulation across grade levels. Vertical teams usually consist of teachers from the same subject-matter area. If the area is mathematics, for example, teachers of mathematics from different grade levels might meet periodically to make certain that students are being taught the prerequisites to do well at each succeeding grade level. Vertical teams engage in developing curricula, troubleshooting student weaknesses, ordering instructional materials, and organizing staff development.

Another component of a school's organizational structure can be a special team designed to intervene when students are falling seriously behind in their work. Such teams engage in diagnosing student academic problems, planning corrective strategies, and implementing these strategies. Intervention teams can be particularly important when students are struggling in a number of subjects.

Two other examples of structural arrangements are school improvement committees and leadership teams. Both constitute decision-making bodies consisting of elected or appointed faculty representatives and administrators. These groups often set improvement targets, monitor progress toward achieving the targets, and allocate resources. They also may become involved in organizing staff development activities, handling school crises, and selecting new staff members.

Without these kinds of structural arrangements, collaboration and cooperation become extremely difficult. Teachers and administrators are busy people. In the absence of defined groups with specific charges and scheduled meeting times, people are apt to go their separate ways, taking care of their own business and complaining about the lack of coordination and common commitment. We have not encountered one school turnaround success in which teachers and administrators worked largely on their own. If arrangements for collaboration and cooperation are not in place in your school, the establishment of such arrangements definitely should be addressed during the planning process.

Bear in mind, however, that having teams and committees in place is only the first step to promoting collaboration and cooperation. These groups must develop processes for handling their business efficiently and dealing with difficult issues in an open and honest way. The effectiveness of teams and committees is often contingent on the nature of a school's organizational culture.

Organizational Culture

The elements of school culture that contribute to low performance already have been noted. The absence of arrangements for teacher teams and leadership groups often indicates a culture in which little value is placed on cooperation. The following description captures features of a positive school culture, one that is likely to enhance efforts to raise student achievement:

A school . . . culture that is supportive of change is characterized by the expectation that teachers and administrators continually search for new and better ways to promote effective teaching and learning. Improvement is valued in such a culture, and norms encourage individuals and groups to question traditional practice and challenge assumptions about what, where, when, and how to learn. (Duke 2004, 133).

In order to assess the extent to which a school's culture is receptive to improvement, Duke (2004, 134) offers several illustrative questions:

1. Are teachers and administrators expected to continually search for new and better ways to teach and learn?
2. Is a positive value placed on experimentation, improvement, and reform?
3. Do teachers and administrators feel free to question current policies, programs, and practices?

4. Are new ideas and divergent views greeted with an open mind and a desire to understand?

Some individuals are apt to associate a constructive school culture with shared values, and, to a certain extent, they are correct. But when an emphasis on shared values leads to the criticism or exclusion of anyone with divergent views, a school runs the risk of "groupthink." Originally described by Irving Janis (1972), groupthink occurs when organization members are more interested in preserving comfortable relationships with each other than they are in arriving at sound decisions. Sound decisions sometimes require people to question conventional wisdom and raise "difficult" questions.

> *Turnaround Trap:* Individuals engaged in assessing a school's culture should be careful about the appearance of strongly shared values. It may be an indication of groupthink.

While school culture can be a critical component of a school's capacity for change, culture itself is not easily changed! The rule of thumb goes like this—if it can be easily changed, it's not culture. By its very nature, the culture of a school represents those values, beliefs, and assumptions that are stable and enduring. If you determine that your school's culture is contributing to low performance, you must recognize that any effort to improve the culture will require time, patience, and persistence.

Resources

The third element of a school's capacity for change involves resources. Two resources are of primary importance in achieving school turnaround—time and money. And since time must be reimbursed, except in the case of volunteers, resources boil down to money. Change is not cheap, especially when the focus is overcoming a track record of low performance. A partial list of some of the additional expenses associated with the school turnaround process includes the following items:

- New reading and mathematics programs
- New textbooks and supplementary instructional materials
- Staff development
- Stipends for teachers engaged in preturnaround planning activities

- Improvements in school facilities
- Additional technology, including up-to-date computers and software for administrative, instructional, and data management purposes
- Visits to schools that have successfully turned around
- Recruitment of highly qualified teachers to fill vacancies
- Reading and/or math specialists
- Additional teachers to lower teacher-student ratios
- Afterschool and extended learning time programs
- Special summer programs for struggling students
- Tutors for students

Any effort to assess the availability of adequate resources for school improvement must involve school district administrators. Some school systems also have foundations that serve as conduits for private donations to help defray the cost of improvement projects. Additional resources may be obtained from state and federal grants, private philanthropic organizations, and local businesses.

Determining the additional resources required to turn around a low-performing school should not focus only on planning and the first year of the initiative. The need for staff development, for example, is ongoing. When new teachers are hired, they will need the same training that the faculty received prior to launching the turnaround process. It is impossible, of course, to anticipate all the possible needs for additional resources. A firm agreement with school district officials and other funders to set aside sufficient resources to support school turnaround for at least three years is therefore crucial. Few things are more frustrating and dispiriting than getting off to a promising start with school improvement efforts, only to discover that funds to continue the process are no longer available.

What Are the Priorities on Which Teachers Should Focus?

Just because a low-performing school is plagued by a plethora of problems is no excuse for compounding matters by trying to address every problem simultaneously. Such a course of action is almost certain to produce disappointment, frustration, and failure. What a low-performing school needs most is confidence, and confidence comes from success. Success at first need not be across the board. A few well-targeted "victories" can generate the needed confidence and esprit de corps to tackle additional problems. The desired effect is comparable to a snowball rolling downhill, gathering momentum and growing in size as it goes.

Where to begin, that is the question. Many successful turnaround specialists have found it beneficial to create a very focused mission statement. The mission statement tells everyone what a school intends to do to turn itself around. A mission statement need not be a dull dollop of bureaucratic jargon. When Deloris Crews and the teachers at Glenwood Elementary School in Danville, Virginia, initiated their school turnaround program, they looked at their students' scores on the state's fifth-grade reading test and decided they needed to focus first on raising the passing rate. While they had no intention of neglecting other grade levels, they agreed that job one was ensuring that fifth graders received the reading instruction they needed to pass the state test and subsequently succeed in middle school.

The Glenwood staff expressed their mission in the form of a catchy slogan: "Doing Your Best, Wildcats Achieve Success 31/48." The wildcat was Glenwood's mascot. The number 31 represented the percentage increase in students passing the state's fifth-grade reading test that was needed to meet Virginia's benchmark passing rate of 75 percent. The number 48 represented the number of staff members at Glenwood. Not just teachers working with fifth graders. The entire Glenwood staff. The slogan made it clear that it would take the efforts of every staff member to raise the reading achievement of fifth graders.

A number of low-performing schools experience problems with student attendance and discipline. Reducing absenteeism and behavior problems therefore may be priority goals for a school struggling to raise student achievement. It is hard for students to learn, after all, when they are not in school and when their classes are constantly being disrupted. Goals related to attendance and orderliness are not a substitute, though, for goals involving student achievement. We recommend that mission statements place academic achievement at the forefront.

Turnaround Tip: A good mission statement for a low-performing school is one that targets improvements in academic achievement.

Michael Fullan (2006, 45) suggests building a school mission around the goal of "raising the bar and closing the gap." "Raising the bar" involves increasing expectations for student achievement. He reasons that focusing on getting students to meet minimum academic requirements will be of little value when students eventually have to compete for admission to a good college or a good job. "Closing the gap" refers to reducing the differences between high-achieving and low-achieving students.

Once a focused mission statement has been agreed upon, teachers should identify the specific steps required to accomplish the mission. Formalizing these steps by adopting a data management system like the Balanced Scorecard (Kaplan and Norton 1996) or creating a system is important. Without a system to help with the monitoring of school progress, it is too easy for teachers to get caught up in the daily challenges of teaching and lose sight of where they and their students are supposed to be headed. We have seen schools in which the high-minded mission that was developed in August is displaced by November, when just getting to the weekend without a major problem becomes the "unofficial" mission. By February, if teachers are not vigilant, the real objective may be just getting through the day without a disaster.

> *Turnaround Trap:* When we allow weekly and daily concerns to displace yearlong goals, achieving a school's turnaround mission is unlikely.

Schools participating in the School Turnaround Specialist Program receive extensive training in the development and use of the Balanced Scorecard. A key element in planning for a successful school turnaround involves creating a committee of teachers and administrators to develop strategic objectives for the school's Balanced Scorecard. For each strategic objective, the committee identifies (a) one or more "measures" to be used in determining when the objective has been achieved and (b) quarterly benchmarks to help with monitoring progress. One individual on the staff is designated to be responsible for monitoring progress on each strategic objective. A school's Balanced Scorecard is revised each year in light of the preceding year's track record.

The success of the Balanced Scorecard, or any other data management system, is a function of the specificity and scope of the objectives. Listed below is an objective that was developed for one of the elementary schools in the School Turnaround Specialist Program. It illustrates how specific and precise an objective and its related measures need to be.

Strategic Objective 1.1: Utilize a comprehensive Reading Model, complete with curriculum material, scope, sequence, and schedule.

Measure 1.1.1. Date when 100 percent of teachers are fully trained on the Reading Model and curriculum material.

Measure 1.1.2. Date when a fully complete scope and sequence for each grade level and content area is available to all teachers.

Measure 1.1.3. Percent of teachers on scope and sequence for reading.

Measure 1.1.4. Percent of students showing mastery on formative assessment tool for reading for each grade.

Specific objectives and measures provide teachers with an unambiguous view of where the school needs to go in order to raise student achievement. Individuals who dislike or feel uncomfortable focusing on such details may not be well-suited to the challenges associated with turning around a low-performing school. The schools that we have observed raising student achievement all have focused on specific objectives and monitored progress on a regular basis over the course of the school year.

Are Teachers Ready, Willing, and Able to Undertake the School Turnaround Process?

School turnaround is a process that takes place at an organizational level, but "successful change starts and ends at the individual level" (Hall and Hord 2006, 7). It is teachers who must accept and embrace the idea that change is necessary. Most of the actual work of any school improvement initiative must be done with and by teachers, and without their willingness to reconsider and possibly alter their actual practices, these efforts will fail. Before the turnaround process can begin, teachers need to ask themselves and their colleagues the following questions:

1. Are we ready to acknowledge that students are not as successful as they could be?
2. Are we willing to do what it takes to improve teaching and learning in the school?
3. Are we able to make the needed changes in policies, practices, and programs?

Readiness to Change

In the case of many schools that are low performing, typically there has been some recognition of problems by teachers and administrators, but responses tend to be piecemeal and incremental, such as a new reading program or an afterschool program. Evidence of schoolwide change is elusive, in part, due to avoidance of the broader issues, complacency with existing policies and practices, and uncertainty about how to proceed. Without a visible crisis or external pressure, it is easier to accept the status quo. Teachers may feel that they are working incredibly hard already, and there are limits to their ability to improve the achievement of some students. Until teachers acknowledge the urgency of raising student performance, there is insufficient impetus for the challenging and unsettling work of wide-scale change (Kotter 1996).

In today's climate of educational accountability, a sense of urgency may be created by the state or school district. If schools fail to make adequate yearly progress for three years, they can be declared "in need of improvement." Sanctions vary from state to state. A new principal may be hired or an academic review team may visit and generate a list of recommendations for curricular and instructional improvement. Some schools are even reconstituted, an action which requires teachers and staff to reapply for their positions. At Greenfield Elementary School, which was introduced in chapter 2, the teachers did not realize that they had lost their state accreditation and had not made adequate yearly progress until they returned to the school in late August. No one had shared the testing results with them. Many teachers heard the bad news as a call to action.

> *Turnaround Tip:* Use state and federal accountability standards as leverage for creating a sense of urgency for change.

Complacency with existing conditions is understandable and to be expected when performance data is unavailable. Until a faculty fully understands the extent of problems and their implications, little readiness to undertake change can be expected. As a result, external forces and performance data can be powerful tools for producing the openness that characterizes readiness. Sometimes, though, problems are recognized by teachers but they blame colleagues, parents, or even students for underachievement. In one study of an underperforming high school, 57 percent of the teachers blamed the students for underachievement, and 64 percent blamed the parents (Thompson, Warren, and Carter 2004). All of these parties need to be seen as allies in the collective enterprise of addressing problems. In the turnaround schools that we have studied, teachers report that, in some cases, a grassroots approach to "selling" the turnaround process to fellow teachers is often necessary to convince them to "get on board" with improvement initiatives. Typical is one fifth-year teacher who described her role in the school turnaround process this way: "I feel like I'm a team player and I feel like I encourage people to be team players as well. I think I have been pretty positive and I think that maybe it helps encourage others who are feeling down or are reluctant to be a part of the turnaround process. I think that my positive attitude has helped move people in the right direction." Not everyone recognizes the need for change at the same time, nor do they share a similar enthusiasm for the work, but meaningful change cannot begin without a critical mass of faculty agreeing that there is a problem and that action must be taken.

Willingness to Change

A willingness to change involves the explicit intent to take action and is rooted deeply in teacher beliefs and attitudes that their actions will make a difference. Teacher beliefs about students drive their decisions about every aspect of teaching and influence their expectations of students. These expectations can both enhance and hinder student performance. Most common is the "self-fulfilling prophecy effect," which entails expectations about people that influence behavior in such a way that they respond in the expected way. Self-fulfilling prophecies can be both positive and negative. Positive prophecies have a more powerful effect than negative ones, and both types have a greater effect on low achievers than high achievers. Teachers communicate their expectations in various ways, including grouping practices, feedback and evaluation practices, and motivational strategies. In response to the expectations communicated through such practices, students develop beliefs about their own potential as learners (Good and Brophy 2003). Although teachers may be unaware of their differential expectations for students, they can have a tremendous influence on student performance.

It is true that beliefs influence expectations for students, but research on teacher beliefs also indicates that "[b]elief systems are dynamic and permeable mental structures, susceptible to change in light of experience. The relationship between beliefs and practice is also not a simple one-way relationship from belief to practice, but a dynamic two-way relationship in which beliefs are influenced by practical experience" (Muijs and Reynolds 2002, 4). This understanding of beliefs suggests that positive experiences can change beliefs about the abilities of students to learn and serve as an impetus to improved performance. If teachers can create opportunities for students to demonstrate their potential for academic growth, these experiences can lead to changes in beliefs about what is possible in low-performing schools.

> *Turnaround Trap:* Low academic expectations for children can become self-fulfilling prophecies.

In our study of turnaround schools, teachers espouse strong beliefs about three major topics: the change process, working with their colleagues, and student learning. These individual beliefs underpin the school culture and determine the norms and practices that take place in a school. Beliefs are "powerful in schools because they represent the core understandings about student capacity, teacher responsibility for learning, expert sources of teacher knowledge, and educational success" (Deal and Peterson 1999, 27). Teachers in successful turnaround schools often agree on core ideas, such as the necessity of continuous improvement, the effectiveness of teamwork, and the importance of high expectations for students.

The first set of beliefs that teachers need to confront for school turnaround are those related to the need for change. Change tends to create anxiety in most people, and questions immediately arise about how it will impact them. What will it mean for individual teachers? Will it affect how the school functions? Some measure of caution is healthy, but often reasons such as a commitment to the status quo, a lack of awareness about the reasons for change, the potential for disruption and discomfort, and an anticipated increase in workload lead to overt resistance to any change. While resistance is to be expected throughout the turnaround process, it is most common during the planning stage (Duke 2004). This may be due to the fact that the potential drawbacks to the change process are easily imagined whereas the potential rewards and successes are less tangible. When only 40 percent of your students are passing the third grade reading test, it's hard to believe that 80 percent could pass with a restructured reading program. It is far easier to foresee increased pressure on the third-grade teachers to produce results.

With innovation in any field, people tend to fall along a continuum of enthusiasm for change efforts. Hall and Hord (2006), two prominent researchers on change, categorize people into the following five types: innovators, early adopters, early majority, late majority, and laggards. Each group has distinct characteristics and varying levels of leadership and status within an organization. The more secure and confident people are, the more willing they are to consider change. As you plan for school turnaround, you want to identify innovators who enjoy entertaining new ideas and are willing to give them a try. Getting innovators on board early helps to build the central core of the leadership team needed to facilitate change. This group then needs to appeal to a broader group of early adopters who tend to be highly respected members of the faculty, but who are more cautious in their adoption of new ideas. Together these two groups can provide the critical mass of teachers needed to persuade other teachers to support a new initiative.

Turnaround Tip: Find teachers who enjoy new ideas and recruit them to be part of the initial planning team for school turnaround.

No matter how well you plan your efforts to persuade other teachers of the importance of undertaking change, personal and professional adjustments will be necessary. One third-grade teacher with five years of experience shared her experience: "I think in the very beginning [the turnaround process] was kind of overwhelming but as time has gone by, it has kind of become routine and I think everything is okay. I just went with [the turnaround process], and the more I was exposed to it and involved with it, the less overwhelmed I became and [the turnaround practices] became habit."

Once individuals are willing to consider change, they must accept the need to work as a team. Literature from both the business and education worlds speaks to the power of teams to achieve remarkable results. Thomas Edison, in explaining the productivity of his Menlo Park laboratory, called the phenomenon the "multiplier effect." Instead of working in isolation, he had his scientists working in teams to share their collective knowledge and new findings. He was convinced that they were more productive when working in large laboratories where there was sharing of ideas and insights. In a similar fashion, teamwork offers an opportunity for groups of teachers to share and develop their "intellectual capital" around specific problems of practice.

Given the challenges faced by turnaround schools, teamwork is essential to coordinate planning and instruction within and across grade levels. Research has found that more effective schools are characterized by teachers who work together to share ideas and discuss strategies to improve student learning (Good and Brophy 2003). A third-grade teacher explained the role of collaboration in a turnaround school: "We collaborate with each other in planning and are really focused on looking at our weaknesses and thinking about ways to strengthen those weaknesses in our school improvement plan. Teamwork, too, is very helpful. It kind of helps to see that we don't have to do everything by ourselves; we have a team here. I think it almost makes our jobs easier." Educators, too, can enjoy Edison's multiplier effect, if collaboration is supported and encouraged through organizational structures, such as common planning time, and through the school culture.

How teachers feel about student learning constitutes a third set of beliefs and values that seem to be foundational to their ability to embrace schoolwide changes. Two very basic beliefs were discussed by almost every teacher with whom we spoke.

1. All students can learn.
2. Teachers must set high expectations for students.

As obvious as these ideas may sound, teachers in our study repeatedly report how important they are to school success. Typical is one third-grade teacher (in her fifth year of teaching) who observed, "This probably sounds so silly, but all children *can* learn and it doesn't matter what kind of background kids have or what's going on in their lives. You have control of what you can do during the school day. It [school turnaround] can happen." Nationwide, 80 percent of teachers claim to believe all children can learn (MetLife 2001), and this belief holds true regardless of the income level and minority status of the students with whom a teacher works. Although beliefs do not automatically translate into actions, they do provide common ground on which educators can plan for school turnaround.

High academic expectations for students are another mainstay of school improvement efforts (Good and Brophy 2003), and yet surveys of teachers suggest that only about half agree that there are high expectations for all students in their schools. For schools with a majority of minority students, the percentage drops even further to 40 percent. Similar results are found when teachers are asked how challenging the curriculum is in their school. Only 41 percent of teachers in the poorest schools strongly agree that the curriculum challenges students. Paradoxically, a much higher percentage of teachers (66%) strongly agree that if teachers have high academic expectations, students will rise to meet them (MetLife 2001). This finding suggests that teachers believe that students will rise to the occasion if only teachers would raise the bar.

Given the conditions that exist in many communities where low-performing schools are located, immediate concerns such as food, clothing, shelter, and safety can and do distract educators from academics. High expectations for achievement sometimes may seem unfair or unrealistic. External academic standards can provide leverage in these circumstances to reinforce the importance of educational priorities. As one counselor and former teacher observed, "We can't make excuses because 98 percent of the students are on free or reduced-price lunch, the standards [for achievement] are still the same." This logic is the bedrock of improvement efforts in turnaround schools and must be part of the commitment to the planning process.

Ability to Change

Readiness and willingness to change are necessary but not sufficient conditions for teachers to begin the turnaround process. As noted earlier, meeting the needs of diverse learners requires professional knowledge in many areas, including student learning, content knowledge, pedagogy, and assessment techniques. Individual teachers may lack the necessary knowledge and skills to design and implement changes to improve the quality of learning in their classrooms despite a desire to do so. It is often easier and less revealing of possible weaknesses to simply request additional special services rather than to change basic classroom instruction, and yet we know that the classroom is where instructional improvement can have the greatest impact.

> *Turnaround Trap:* Don't underestimate the need for additional training and/or coaching to address the diverse needs of students in turnaround schools.

The ability of teachers to change can be influenced by new knowledge. According to Mary Kennedy, in her book *Inside Teaching* (2005), teachers acquire knowledge through informal, institutional, and knowledge-vending sources. Informal sources include personal experience and professional work with colleagues. Assessment systems and curriculum guides constitute primary institutional sources of knowledge, and professional development programs are a primary knowledge-vending source. All of the above can be powerful sources of new knowledge, and they need to be considered in an overall plan for building the skills needed by a faculty to improve teaching and learning. The more closely aligned they are with the reform efforts within a school, the more beneficial they can be in enabling faculty to undertake change.

Is There Any Benefit in Adopting an Established Improvement Program?

Schools desiring to improve have at least three options. They can develop their own approach, adopt an existing reform program, or adapt such a program to their own unique circumstances. An enormous range of options exists. Some programs focus on only one element of school improvement. The Core Knowledge program, representing E. D. Hirsch's work on "cultural literacy," focuses primarily on essential curriculum content. Commercial programs that target reading, mathematics, and classroom management skills also are available for teachers in low-performing schools. Other programs are truly comprehensive. Robert Slavin's Success for All encompasses curriculum materials, instructional strategies, provisions for student grouping, and adjustments to school organization. Many comprehensive programs come with implementation manuals, consulting services, and staff development. Comprehensive programs got a boost in 1994 when the law regarding Title I was changed to make it easier for high-poverty schools to become schoolwide Title I projects. This change meant that Title I schools could undertake reforms that benefited all students, not just those who previously qualified for assistance.

Should you and your colleagues choose to consider adopting or adapting an established program, there are several things to consider. Cost is an obvious consideration. Some reading and math programs and comprehensive school improvement programs carry hefty price tags. Besides instructional materials and initial training, schools may be required to contract for ongoing services to ensure that the program is implemented correctly. Another consideration is the amount of time required for training and implementation. It also is essential to find out where the program has previously been implemented and with what degree of success. If high-quality research and evaluation studies have been conducted on a program, this material should be obtained and carefully reviewed. Be sure to find out whether studies were conducted by impartial individuals. Do not be surprised if the program has been found to work in some places but not in others. Two comprehensive programs that have been studied a great deal and found to be effective in many schools are the Comer School Development Program and Success for All from Johns Hopkins University (Fashola and Slavin 1998).

Most programs embody certain key assumptions. The Comer School Development Program, developed by Yale child psychiatrist James Comer and adopted by hundreds of schools across the United States, is based on the premise that good educational practice is rooted in an understanding of child and adolescent development (Comer 2004). The Comer program further assumes that learning is a function of the relationships between students and the adults in a school. If teachers do not accept the assumptions supporting a program, it may not be wise to adopt it, even if certain program components are appealing. Many programs, especially comprehensive ones like the Comer program, depend on teachers embracing all elements, not picking and choosing the elements that they like. There is a long history of failed reforms in public schools that can be traced to the reluctance of educators to implement programs as their developers intended.

The likelihood of teachers taking ownership of an improvement program probably is greatest if they are involved in developing their own set of reforms. Some aspects of school improvement, of course, are more likely to benefit from local development than others. The time and resources required for a faculty to create a new reading series, for example, probably would be prohibitive. Designing an extended day program involving local teachers and community volunteers, on the other hand, is well within the capacity of a school's faculty.

Regardless of whether a school adopts, adapts, or designs a school turnaround program, the likelihood of success is enhanced by considering a variety of alternatives. No matter how powerful the sales pitch for a particular program, educators should resist the temptation to jump on the first bandwagon they see. A school turnaround program is most likely to be effective when it is carefully matched to the needs of students, the beliefs and abilities of teachers, and the culture of the school and school system.

> *Turnaround Trap:* Choosing the first program that promises impressive achievement gains is a risky way to plan a school turnaround initiative.

FOLLOW-UP ACTIVITIES

1. A key part of planning for school turnaround is determining what kinds of staff development will be required. In this regard it can be beneficial to contact another school that already has embarked on the process of school improvement and find out what kinds of staff development were most and least helpful.

2. While it is often necessary to obtain staff development providers from outside your school, you should not overlook the expertise within your faculty. Prior to launching your school turnaround process, determine what specialized training has been received by teachers at your school and their willingness to share it.

3. Before beginning the actual planning of a school turnaround initiative, it may be helpful to undertake a trial run. Choose a very specific objective, such as "raising the level of student comprehension of reading material in the third grade." Survey your fellow teachers regarding what they would do to address the objective. To what extent do people agree about how to improve reading comprehension? You also may want to survey teachers at another school, one where reading performance is higher.

REFERENCES

Comer, James P. 2004. *Leave No Child Behind*. New Haven, CT: Yale.

Deal, Terrence E., and Kent D. Peterson, 1999. *Shaping School Culture: The Heart of Leadership*. San Francisco: Jossey-Bass.

Duke, Daniel L. 2004. *The Challenges of Educational Change*. Boston: Pearson.

Duke, Daniel L., et. al. 2005. *Lift-off: Launching the School Turnaround Process in Virginia Schools*. Charlottesville, VA: Partnership for Leaders in Education, University of Virginia.

Fashola, Olatokunbo S., and Robert E. Slavin. 1998. "School Reform Models: What Works?" *Phi Delta Kappan* 80(5): 370–79.

Fullan, Michael. 2006. *Turnaround Leadership*. San Francisco: Jossey-Bass.

Good, Thomas L., and Jere E. Brophy. 2003. *Looking in Classrooms*. 9th ed. Boston: Allyn & Bacon.

Hall, Gene E., and Shirley M. Hord. 2006. *Implementing Change: Patterns, Principles and Potholes*. Boston: Pearson.

Janis, Irving. 1972. *Victims of Groupthink*. Boston: Houghton Mifflin.

Johnson, Joseph F., and Rose Asera, eds. 1999. *Hope for Urban Education: A Study of Nine High-Performing, High-Poverty, Urban Elementary Schools*. Austin: Charles A. Dana Center, University of Texas.

Kaplan, Robert S., and David P. Norton. 1996. "Using the Balanced Scorecard as a Strategic Management System." *Harvard Business Review*, 1–11 (reprint).

Kennedy, Mary M. 2005. *Inside Teaching: How Classroom Life Undermines Reform*. Cambridge, MA: Harvard University Press.

Kotter, John P. 1996. *Leading Change*. Boston: Harvard Business School Press.

MetLife. 2001. *The MetLife Survey of the American Teacher 1001: Key Elements of Quality Schools*. Hartford, CT: Author.

Muijs, Daniel, and David Reynolds. 2002. "Teachers' Beliefs and Behaviors: What Really Matters." *Journal of Classroom Interaction* 37(2): 3–15.

Opening Doors: Promising Lessons from Five Texas High Schools. 2001. Austin: Charles A. Dana Center, University of Texas.

Picucci, A. C., Amanda Brownson, Rahel Kahlert, and Andrew Sobel. 2002. *Driven to Succeed: High-Performing, High-Poverty, Turnaround Middle Schools*. Austin: Charles A. Dana Center, University of Texas.

The Power to Change: High Schools that Help All Students Achieve. 2005. Washington, DC: Education Trust.

Thompson, Gail L., Susan Warren, and LaMesha Carter. 2004. "It's Not My Fault: Predicting High School Teachers Who Blame Parents and Students' Low Achievement." *High School Journal* 87(3): 5–14.

6

The First Year of the School Turnaround Process

School turnaround at Woodville Elementary School in Richmond, Virginia, began with a faculty retreat to discuss shared beliefs as educators, student achievement scores, and future directions for the school. Teachers gathered a week before school officially began to talk about their school and the children who attended it. They shared their concerns about the present and hopes for the future. Common goals were agreed upon and enthusiasm was generated for the beginning of the school year. Thoughtful planning by the leadership team, as described in the previous chapter, made this experience a success for everyone involved, including custodians, office support, and cafeteria workers. The aspirations voiced by teachers and staff at this retreat gave people the motivation to face the challenges of the first year with a sense of purpose.

In this chapter, we offer guidance on common approaches taken in the turnaround schools we have studied, but we acknowledge that no two turnaround paths are the same. Planning for systemic change is essential, but the process will unfold in a manner that reflects the individual school context. Since no two underperforming schools exhibit the same set of problems or circumstances, change must be responsive to the set of policies, programs, and practices that exist within the school and the people who make up its community. Some schools are located in rural communities and others in urban centers. Some are well resourced, but unfortunately, many are not. Given the range of schools that might undertake a turnaround effort, it would be unwise to suggest that the interpersonal considerations and high-yield strategies we describe exhaust the possible responses to a given situation, but they are a start. We encourage you to shape these ideas to your situation.

> *Turnaround Tip:* No two low-performing schools are identical, and as a result, there is no one way to turn around a low-performing school.

BRIDGING PLANNING AND ACTION

The organic nature of change makes it difficult to demarcate clearly the line between planning and action because each informs the other, creating a cyclical process that takes place over time. The issues discussed in the planning section, such as organizational structure, organizational culture, and resources, need to be revisited regularly if ongoing improvements are to be made. For example, teachers may request professional development to implement a new reading series that has been adopted. As a consequence, resources would need to be reallocated in order to provide the necessary training to ensure this curricular change is implemented with fidelity. Each of the considerations in the planning process continues to be relevant as the change effort unfolds.

During the first year of school turnaround, there are two aspects of the change process that must be considered and addressed simultaneously to be successful. On the one hand are the high-yield strategies that are associated with meaningful school improvement and on the other hand is the interpersonal work with constituencies. The high-yield strategies are more structural and technical in nature while the interpersonal work is more social and political in nature. Both are integral to any effort to bring about change. High-yield strategies involve the "what" of school change while interpersonal dimensions define the "how." In this chapter, the primary focus will be on the high-yield strategies that we are finding to be universal across successful turnaround schools, but we begin with a discussion of what Evans (1996) calls the "human side of change."

INTERPERSONAL DIMENSIONS OF CHANGE

The "how" of school change is different for every school, but there are some key tasks that bridge the planning and implementation stages to which we alluded in chapter 5 and highlight here. These tasks focus on developing meaning and working with the existing culture to bring about the needed changes. They are described by John Kotter (1996), who writes about change in the business world and whose work mirrors what we have found in turnaround schools. He argues that failing to attend to each of the following activities has the potential to undermine and derail new initiatives. If there are essential elements in implementing major changes, the list below probably captures them.

1. Establish a sense of urgency.
2. Create a guiding coalition.
3. Develop a vision and strategy.
4. Communicate the change vision.
5. Empower broad-based action.

Teachers with whom we spoke alluded to each of these stages as they described the first few months of the turnaround process. The relevance of these tasks for schools is clear, and they serve to create and communicate the meaning of change to those who must implement it. Sometimes the initial stages of this work take place during the summer as part of a formal planning process, but more often, they occur during the initial weeks and months of school turnaround.

Establishing a Sense of Urgency

Without a sense of urgency about the need for change on the part of teachers, it is unlikely that the most valuable resource within a school, its faculty, will be mobilized. In the schools we have studied, the superintendent or school board typically sets the stage for creating a sense of urgency for change by pointing to alarming data on student achievement. It is then up to the principal, who may be newly appointed, to make the case for change. This involves being brutally honest about student achievement and its possible consequences if learning, and therefore teaching, does not improve. Change also involves understanding why achievement is low. Sara Jamison at Greenfield Elementary School recognized that she had to listen to the stories of her teachers about the conditions in the school during the years preceding her appointment before they could discuss the future. There had to be an acknowledgment by teachers that they needed help in moving forward and a recognition that the new principal could provide it before the teachers agreed that the need for change was urgent.

Creating a Guiding Coalition

If there is a single component that makes turnaround schools successful, it is the coalition of influential teachers in each school who are willing to embrace schoolwide change as a real possibility. The cultivation of leadership teams is critical to the turnaround process because their members facilitate the interpersonal side of change. They model teamwork and the collaborative orientation that is necessary for developing a positive and supportive school culture. The willingness of the team members to try new ideas and take risks creates an environment that encourages innovation and new learning. They also serve as key communicators with other faculty and staff within the building, making the change process as transparent as possible and involving everyone in it. They encourage the formation of grade-level and content-area teams throughout the school and encourage others to work together by supporting them with the necessary time and structures for success.

Developing a Vision and a Strategy

Without a vision and a strategy for change, there is no focus or direction for individuals who are interested in change. Prior to school turnarounds, some teachers are likely to have left due to frustrations over a lack of direction and common goals. An important function of the leadership team early in the turnaround process is the creation of a vision for the school and identification of strategies for achieving the vision. People who know the school and its community are in the best position to imagine the future and the meaning it will have. A new principal cannot do this without the input of others. Once there is agreement on a vision, priorities and goals can be established that provide a compass for aligning the high-yield strategies discussed later in this chapter.

Communicating the Change Vision

The leadership team is pivotal in giving direction to the turnaround process and creating early momentum, but other faculty members must be encouraged to participate in the change process. This is accomplished through relentless communication of the big ideas. Communication is important because the "shared sense of a desirable future can help motivate and coordinate the kinds of actions that create transformations" (Kotter 1996, 85). The message can be communicated formally in meetings, memos, and slogans, and informally through social networks within the school. The leadership team plays a key role in persuading colleagues that changes are necessary for the sake of students, the school, and the community. They often appeal to the values and beliefs of their colleagues about the role of education in the lives of children. Lastly, opportunities for dialogue and processing of ideas facilitate ongoing communication that keeps everyone involved and informed about the process. At some points, efforts also must be made to persuade other constituencies, such as support staff and parents, to support reform.

Turnaround Tip: Complex change involves consideration of both the technical aspects of implementation and the people who will implement it.

Empowering Broad-Based Action

Without the support systems to empower broad-based action, the necessary momentum for change cannot be achieved. The high-yield strategies discussed in the next section constitute what we have found to be critical sources of support for school change. They include alignment of curriculum, instruction, and assessment; alignment of resources with goals; instructionally focused teacher teams; targeted professional development; benchmark testing; reduction of discipline problems; and family engagement. Many school improvement efforts include one or more of these strategies, but we have found that school turnaround requires more broad-based efforts to support comprehensive change. The more strategies that are used and the more closely aligned they are, the more successful school turnaround will be.

HIGH-YIELD STRATEGIES FOR SCHOOL TURNAROUND

School turnaround requires thoughtful reflection and hard work on the part of all school personnel. Existing conditions must be assessed, plans must be developed for how to begin the change process, resources must be mobilized, and then action must be taken. Of course, change rarely proceeds in a linear fashion, and there is a constant back and forth between planning and action. As you consider what actions to take and where to put your energy, the following list of high-yield strategies is a good place to begin. Based on our research and that of others studying school reform, these strategies have the potential for leveraging gains in student learning. Each one will be discussed along with illustrative examples from Greenfield Elementary School.

1. Program review and alignment
2. Alignment of time, people, and other resources with academic goals
3. Instructionally focused teacher teams
4. Monitoring of student learning
5. Targeted professional development
6. Reduction of behavior problems and absenteeism
7. Family and community involvement

Program Review and Alignment

One of the initial steps that must be taken when a school is underperforming is a comprehensive program review. This step begins in the planning stage but becomes a continuous process throughout the first year and beyond. What is working well and what is not? Student achievement data can offer some clues as to problem areas, but a general discussion among faculty provides far richer and more specific information. The reading or language arts program is a good place to start because most underperforming schools have low reading achievement. Possible questions to be explored are the following:

1. Is there a formal curriculum with pacing guides that is followed by all teachers?
2. Is the curriculum aligned with state standards and assessments?
3. Is the curriculum delivered using research-based instructional strategies?
4. Are necessary resources available such as up-to-date texts for all students, math manipulatives, and current maps?

In many underperforming schools, there are major gaps in the curriculum when it is compared to the state standards and assessments. If children are not taught the mandated curriculum, they cannot demonstrate an understanding of it on a test. Typically, content is not sufficiently reviewed and built upon in subsequent years. What is taught in first grade is never covered again, and then the student is tested on it in third grade with poor results. In turnaround schools, substantial teacher meeting time is dedicated to "getting on the same page" so that all students at a particular grade level are taught the same content and the content builds upon concepts that were introduced in previous grades. This alignment and articulation is accomplished through the use of vertical teams (multiple grade levels in the same content area) as well as horizontal teams (multiple content areas on the same grade level).

The purpose of such a program review is to ensure or develop what some researchers refer to as program coherence. Program coherence is defined as "a set of interrelated programs for students and staff that are guided by a common framework for curriculum, instruction, assessment, and learning climate" (Newmann et al. 2001, 297). Studies conducted in Chicago have shown that adoption of coordinated curriculum and assessment efforts that remain stable over time and are supported by appropriate professional development are associated with higher student achievement. Tight alignment of curriculum, instruction, assessment, and professional development brings clarity to what students are expected to know, how teachers will teach it, how teachers and students will know the content has been learned, and how teachers will acquire new learning to inform the instructional process. This level of program coherence should never be assumed to exist, especially in schools where staff turnover is high.

Turnaround Tip: Program coherence is essential to successful school turnaround.

At Greenfield Elementary School, Sara Jamison worked with the faculty to review each content area and examine what was working well, where the gaps were, how resources such as the Title I reading and math specialists could be used to better meet student needs, and what additional resources were needed. There were many instances of excellent teaching and learning within the school, but they were not shared or coordinated in a manner that benefited children across the board. Through the efforts of a small group of interested teachers, dubbed the reading team, a reading curriculum was developed during the first year of turnaround and was formalized in writing during the following summer. New textbooks were purchased as well as book sets that teachers could check out for use in their classrooms. Gaps were identified in the new materials and efforts were made to fill them with supplemental materials. Similar efforts were subsequently undertaken in the other core content areas and special education.

Alignment of Time, People, and Other Resources with Academic Goals

A logical part of the program review process is the identification of available resources and additional ones that may be needed to achieve a school's highly focused academic goals. Time and people tend to be the most valuable resources that schools have available to them, but tangible resources such as textbooks and supplemental materials also are needed to support the academic work of a school. Often these resources are taken for granted and allocated in a manner that is rooted in tradition or is somewhat arbitrary. Common among many schools is the allotment of comparable funds to each teacher within a subject area. This is an equitable approach to resource allocation, but it does not necessarily ensure alignment with overall academic goals. When a faculty has set clear goals, resource purchases can be prioritized and allocated in a more systematic manner that serves the needs of the whole school.

Time is another powerful basis for operationalizing priorities. Many schools, regardless of achievement levels, have dedicated extended blocks in the daily schedule to the core content areas of language arts and math. Given the centrality of these subjects to overall achievement, this is a logical alignment of time with important academic goals. Other schools have expanded the available time in the school week by adding programs for students after school, before school, or on Saturdays. Still other schools have used additional personnel or volunteers to enhance the quality of available time. Reduced class sizes and supplemental tutoring are ways to provide more individualized and intensive instruction within the regular school day.

Teachers and specialists can be assigned or reassigned based on the same agreed-upon priorities. Teaching assignments can be reconsidered in light of whether individuals are teaching to their strengths and whether there are alternative grouping arrangements that would allow greater flexibility in what is taught by whom and when. Once the school, rather than the individual classroom, is seen as the unit of change, many more possible arrangements become apparent. Specialists can support teachers who need assistance by conducting demonstration lessons, coaching, and coteaching. They also can reduce class sizes for targeted subjects, class groups, and specific lessons. The strategic use of support personnel for small reading groups, vocabulary instruction, and group discussion can facilitate the differentiation of instruction that is often required in schools serving students with demanding learning needs.

> *Turnaround Tip:* Resources, especially time and people, should be aligned to support identified school priorities.

Reflecting Greenfield Elementary School's top priority of reading, Title I funding was used to employ an additional reading specialist, instead of a math specialist, because the math program was relatively solid. Reading team members targeted assistance during the first year of school turnaround at the fifth-grade level, where student achievement was the weakest, and then included other grades during the second year of turnaround. Professional development also was provided by the reading team, to supplement training by outside experts. Faculty meetings were organized by teachers to introduce and coordinate the implementation of the newly developed reading program.

Instructionally Focused Teacher Teams

Teacher teams that focused on classroom practice were found in all of the turnaround schools we studied. Typically there was team planning time built into the weekly schedule, permitting regular meetings at the grade level or across content areas. This is yet another example of aligning the resource of time with a school goal of teamwork. Although some schools held team meetings before the turnaround process started, teachers reported that these meetings often were unfocused and unproductive, with little discussion of teaching and learning. Productive team meetings are used to analyze benchmark test data and discern patterns about student learning. These meetings constitute a feedback loop on the effectiveness of the curriculum and various instructional strategies. Teachers exchange ideas about what works and doesn't work with specific lesson plans. Such meetings help to keep teachers on "the same page" of the curriculum pacing guide. Prior experience with instructional strategies and student performance informs future planning. In one turnaround school, a third-grade teacher saw notable changes in the ways teachers worked together:

> I think people have come together and are working within their grade levels as a team as well as working schoolwide as a team. I think our goals have kind of melded into the same ones. Before the turnaround program, this wasn't happening as much. At some grade levels there was that teamwork, and somewhat throughout the school, but I've noticed a huge change over the past few years within my team and the way that we work within the school.

Richard Elmore, a respected author on school reform, observes that in any school, people "specialize or develop particular competencies that are related to their predispositions, interest, aptitudes, prior knowledge, skills, and specialized roles" (2005, 58). To maximize the effectiveness of a school, there needs to be a means to share this expertise and competence so that strengths can be used to complement areas of weakness. Knowledge and skills do not reside in one person or a small group but are recognized as being distributed among all members of a school. The ability to turn a school around requires both contributing to the collective knowledge within the school and recognizing when it is necessary to go outside of the school to obtain what is not readily available. Teachers in successful turnaround schools acknowledge the necessity of teamwork, no matter how challenging it can be, as noted by this kindergarten teacher: "You can't do it on your own. You can't do it by yourself. It does take everybody, and you have to figure out a way to get along and to work together."

Teamwork also serves to improve the delivery of special education in many turnaround schools. When differentiated instruction takes place in regular classrooms, it becomes feasible to include students with disabilities in these classes. Special education teachers then can use collaborative models of service delivery where they plan and work with teachers in the regular classroom to offer small-group instruction for all students who need more intensive support. The teamwork around assistance to students with disabilities ensures exposure to the regular curriculum and benefits other children as well due to the additional adult in the classroom. A special educator commented on the role of collaboration in coordinating services: "I think it's hard sometimes to make sure we're on the same page with what we need to be doing—to make sure that special education students are getting access to the same curriculum that the regular education kids have. Meeting together helps us do this."

> *Turnaround Tip:* Teamwork is the best means of tapping the intellectual capital of the faculty.

Monitoring Student Learning

No individual would undertake a new diet and wait a year to check on his weight, blood sugar, or cholesterol level. The more immediate and specific the feedback, the more influence it has on the behavior you're trying to change. If the feedback is positive, all the better. So it is with a school turnaround. The dramatic individual and collective changes that a school turnaround requires are hard to maintain without feedback that they are making a difference. For this reason, all of the turnaround schools in our studies have implemented benchmark testing every six or nine weeks.

Benchmark testing is a relatively new educational practice that is used to determine student progress toward specific academic goals. Short content-specific assessments are administered to students throughout the year to measure acquisition of knowledge and skills. When this content is mapped against end-of-year learning objectives, it provides a gauge of student progress. A variety of tests exist including commercially developed ones and others that are locally developed by groups of educators. Some tests are administered on a computer for easy scoring and data analysis while others are given using paper and pencil.

For benchmark testing to be used with confidence, the tests should be valid and reliable. Valid tests provide accurate information on student learning of the intended content. They also are a reasonable predictor of performance on end-of-year tests. Some tests may offer useful information on student learning, but if they do not indicate progress toward acquiring required knowledge on end-of-year tests, they do not serve the purpose of benchmark testing. The second important characteristic of benchmark tests is reliability. Reliable tests yield fairly consistent results over time. If scores vary greatly from one administration to the next, they are not helpful for instructional planning purposes. Both validity and reliability of any benchmark test should be considered carefully before adoption.

In addition to their predictive value, benchmark tests provide guidance to teachers for making instructional adjustments in a timely and responsive way. Benchmark tests are considered formative assessments and are not used for student grades. They also provide feedback for grade levels and subject areas about new content needed in the curriculum and the relative emphasis to give curricular goals. Declaring short-term victories with benchmark test results throughout the year can provide much-needed encouragement for students—and teachers—to maintain the necessary effort along the way. Celebrations of these victories add to the sense of purpose and accomplishment of all participants.

Simply implementing benchmark tests, however, is not sufficient for improving learning. As with any test, the data need to be converted into useful information. How this is done is a distinguishing characteristic of successful turnaround schools. As one kindergarten teacher with eighteen years of experience explains, "I think the data is important—not necessarily the testing—but gathering the data and keeping better track of that so you don't let the kids fall between the cracks. You know if a child is getting it or not." To better track student learning, teachers and administrators work together to review test results in depth. In successful schools, they analyze subscales and individual items to identify grade level patterns and individual student weaknesses. Curricular refinements are made, instruction is altered, individualized and small group interventions are developed, and content is reviewed or retaught using a different approach. The test results are not used to make judgments about students, but about the instructional process and how to improve it.

In addition to assessing student academic progress, the testing information is used to determine future learning needs and achievement targets. With regular snapshots of student achievement, teachers can set short- and long-term goals and develop the curriculum content to ensure that students reach grade-level standards. The results from testing inform the instructional program, speeding it up or slowing it down as needed for different groups of students. They also are used to identify individual needs, as this special education teacher noted, "We've become more data driven. We look at each individual student's needs. As part of the school improvement plan, we have individual student plans based on where the kids are weakest in their skills. We have focused more on individual needs."

The monitoring of student progress has been recognized as best practice for decades. Daniel Lortie (1975), in his book on the lives of teachers, noted that monitoring instruction is the heart of *effective* instruction. More recently, the concepts of benchmark testing and the analysis of formative assessment data for instructional planning have become more common. For many teachers it is a new experience to work with data for diagnostic purposes, but one they find valuable. Typical of comments made by many teachers, even relatively young ones, is the following: "The first year, it was a learning process, at least for me. I don't remember having a lot of instruction in college about how to read test data. The way I track the students' progress is a lot better now. I don't think I would have been pushed as much to come up with a way that works if I hadn't been part of this turnaround."

Sara Jamison's experience upon entering Greenfield Elementary School may be typical of more schools than we might expect. Teachers in her school were unaware that they had not met adequate yearly progress under No Child Left Behind until they returned for teacher workdays in late August. They had not seen the dismal test results nor did they understand where they and their students had failed. One of the first professional development days was spent learning how to analyze test results and turn them into useful information for action. The facts were painful and discouraging, but together the teachers were able to rally and devise a plan for school turnaround. They wanted the school to be successful. Guided by information, they were able to set a new course. Their first set of results from benchmark testing confirmed the bad news from the previous year, but by the second round of tests, they began to see progress. By the third round of benchmark tests, parents and students also were clamoring to know the results too. Broad-based investment in the process was taking place and it paid dividends with the tremendous gains that were made in the first year of turnaround at Greenfield.

Turnaround Tip: Change requires new learning for everyone involved.

Targeted Professional Development

To carry out the deep, transformative change that is necessary for school turnaround, instructional personnel need professional development that is targeted to the specific academic goals of the school. There are a variety of mechanisms for creating professional learning opportunities that do not involve traditional in-service workshops. Teachers in turnaround schools describe faculty meetings as occasions when teachers share new instructional ideas and introduce new curricular materials. Team meetings also are spent sharing and critiquing lesson plans, exchanging ideas for teaching particular concepts, and creating pacing guides. This job-embedded learning is relevant, practical, and credible because it is closely aligned with changes taking place within the school.

Although professional development programs tend to be much maligned, research by Mary Kennedy (2005) finds that these programs are the single greatest source of new ideas for classroom teachers. She found that teachers made more substantial changes in their teaching due to professional development programs than they did based on other sources of new knowledge, such as colleagues and their own experiences. They also tended to be more passionate about what was learned as a result of training programs. The area of concern for teachers that was best addressed by professional development was how to foster student learning. This finding speaks to the desire by many teachers to explore new ideas and improve their skills so that they can reach diverse learners in their classrooms.

Professional development in turnaround schools is regarded as another resource to be marshaled for the pursuit of school goals. It is based on program reviews and teacher-identified needs. If classroom-based coaching is needed, the coaching becomes the vehicle for learning. Professional development is broadly defined to include a variety of professional experiences that take place within the context of daily work at the school. It contributes to school improvement in a more tangible way because it is part of a broader effort to redefine and align curriculum, instruction, and assessment. This is in contrast to teachers who may bring a new idea back to their classrooms, only to find that without changes elsewhere in the teaching environment, implementation is impossible. In turnaround schools, there is a reciprocal relationship between the demands of school change and professional development experiences, with each reinforcing the other. The supportive nature of the professional development was described by a kindergarten teacher in one of the turnaround schools. "Over the past two and a half years, I feel like I have been mentored. I've been given staff development that is actually useful and related to what I teach. [The leadership team] has really tried to take all the [turnaround] information and direct it to us and almost hold our hand until we get it."

Turnaround Tip: Professional development should be aligned with specific academic goals for the school.

This grounded approach to professional development was apparent in the way Greenfield Elementary School restructured its special education program. Professional learning was linked to the goal of improving special education services. The special education coordinator from the central office spent considerable time with the newly hired special education team discussing research and reviewing model programs. The team attended a conference on collaborative special education services to learn more about a continuum of placement options for special education. They talked to regular classroom teachers about the types of support needed to help special education students be successful with the regular curriculum. Together with the special education coordinator, the team developed a new service delivery model for the school. Their professional learning resulted in better services for students. Greenfield now offers a range of inclusive options for students with disabilities, not just self-contained classrooms.

Reduction of Behavior Problems and Absenteeism

Concerns about discipline problems existed in a majority of the turnaround schools (68%), particularly at the middle school level, where eight out of nine schools identified this problem as a contributor to the school's low academic performance. Attendance also tended to be a concern in some schools. Teachers often felt that unless student discipline and attendance problems were addressed, they would be unable to improve student achievement. This belief certainly was held by teachers at Greenfield Elementary School.

Sara Jamison responded to this concern during the first month of school by forming a discipline committee. While discipline is often seen as an administrative function, it is actually the role of every adult within the school to remind students of the rules and enforce them consistently. To provide consistency for students throughout a school, it is important that the whole staff perceive the rules as fair and reasonable. In the case of Greenfield Elementary School, a group of teachers developed school-wide rules and a common set of consequences that applied in every classroom. The rules were posted throughout the school and recited every morning as part of the morning announcements. In a matter of weeks, discipline referrals decreased substantially, and fights no longer occurred.

Research (Marzano 2003) suggests that an effective approach to discipline problems is to create a clear set of behavioral expectations for students, enforce them consistently with predictable consequences, and educate students about the meaning of the rules. Sometimes concepts such as "respect" need to be discussed for students to understand the expectations. The manner in which adults treat each other and students sends a powerful message about acceptable behavior within a school. Modeling of desired behavior, therefore, is important. Teachers and staff also need to acknowledge good behavior in addition to sanctioning students who do not follow the rules. Incentives for meeting attendance and behavioral expectations are one strategy used in some schools along with calls to parents when there are problems. When rules are consistently implemented and reinforced, students are more likely to accept them as necessary and beneficial to them and the school as a whole.

Many of the turnaround schools we studied experienced an improvement in discipline and attendance as a secondary gain from their efforts to enhance the instructional program. As teachers were able to focus on a more coherent academic program that was better targeted to students' learning needs, students grew more positive about school. A fourth-grade teacher compared her experience before and after turnaround this way:

> I think students are more excited about coming to school than they may have been before. Discipline problems have gone down because most students will act up if they don't know how to read and if they're not getting [the content]. They love to come to school now. Some of my kids come with fevers because they just don't want to miss any days. So, I think we are doing something [right] that is getting them here.

Family and Community Engagement

Engaging families is particularly difficult for many turnaround schools due to the challenging circumstances many of their families face on a daily basis. Poverty, crime, and unemployment often characterize the communities in which they live. There is a high percentage of single-parent households, and basic necessities are justifiably a greater concern than education. One veteran counselor described her school's challenges as follows. "In this community, where our school is located, there is the lowest education level, highest teen pregnancy rate, and lowest SES and salaries. It's a struggle. There's nothing easy here. We're still dealing with odds people don't want to talk about." When faced with conditions such as these, school counselors, school social workers, and school-community liaisons can be helpful in reaching out to parents in a more affirmative manner by providing transportation to school, contacting homes on a regular basis, and visiting homes as needed.

Despite the difficulties, family engagement remains a high priority in turnaround schools. Research indicates that family involvement is twice as predictive of student academic success as family socioeconomic status and that achievement increases in proportion to the level of family involvement (Epstein et al. 2002). At a very basic level, teachers rely on family members to ensure that students attend school regularly, behave appropriately while in school, and complete homework assignments. Parent support groups can be helpful in fostering some of these behaviors and building trust in what schools are trying to accomplish. Beyond basic parenting tasks, school personnel also encourage regular communication with the home, volunteering within the school, homework assistance, and involvement in school initiatives.

In one school where poverty made the building of a robust Parent Teacher Association difficult, the principal and counselor worked with community partners to provide food and incentives to attract families for evening programs. Teachers planned student performances and workshops to provide engaging activities for the evening get-togethers. Such efforts take a considerable amount of effort but are seen as essential to building bridges with families and the larger community.

Turnaround Tip: Families and communities want the best for their children and will offer support if they see positive changes taking place in their schools.

To offset limited family means, there are numerous options for developing community partnerships that can benefit schools, particularly in urban areas. Alliances can be built with churches, hospitals, health centers, mental health clinics, and housing authorities. These agencies are able to offer free services, educational programs, and volunteers. Some schools work directly with the nearby housing authority to encourage regular school attendance and provide space in which community-based tutoring for students can be offered. School counselors emphasize the importance of getting out into the community and establishing relationships with various organizations to "get people working together." This may be the hardest strategy to implement, as noted by an experienced educator:

> We had to educate the parents who were willing to listen. It took a lot of work: Title I nights at school, going to tenant council meetings, begging parents to be interested in their children. We're still begging parents to come to school, meet with teachers, take responsibility for their children's behavior, and get their kids to school. People who work in schools like this are committed from the heart. Faculty, staff, and the community have to believe in themselves despite the odds.

WORDS OF HOPE

The first year of school turnaround by all accounts is tumultuous. Principals and teachers both report that it is fraught with anxiety, exhaustion, and unexpected gratification. It is analogous to the rapid acceleration of a rocket being launched into orbit around the earth. The liftoff requires a powerful expenditure of energy that defies the forces of gravity and is destabilizing by nature. On the other hand, it is also exhilarating once teachers and students enter orbit and begin to experience success. We found the metaphor of liftoff so apt that we used it for the title of a collection of case studies on the first year of the School Turnaround Program in Virginia (Duke, Tucker, et al. 2005). A description of this work can be found in chapter 9.

Despite the demands of school turnaround, the teachers with whom we have spoken were inspiring and hopeful. There was both pride and weariness in their stories. Their journeys had been challenging, both personally and professionally, but there was a sense of growth and optimism that they had become better teachers and that students were learning more as a result of the struggles. Again, the liftoff analogy matches their experiences. They had been through a dramatic transformation (launch), but many teachers felt they were operating on a higher level (orbit) with more skill and better results. Teachers sensed they were making a difference despite the odds. One veteran fifth-grade teacher simply but elegantly summed up what it takes:

Teachers have to believe in the kids, they have to believe in themselves, and they have to believe as a group that they can get to a common goal if everyone does their part. It's not a "me" thing. It is a "we" thing. Once you get to that point, once you start to believe that, and you have the kids believing in themselves, you'll reach your goal. Everybody in their own little way, even though they would never say it, wanted a change.

FOLLOW-UP ACTIVITIES

1. Is there a "guiding coalition" of teachers in your school? Do members of this group have a clear vision of what they would like to accomplish in your school? Ask each teacher to describe the school in which they would like to work. Is there much agreement among teachers about the characteristics of such a school?

2. Compare current practices in your school with those in the list of high-yield strategies (see Table 6.1). What practices are being implemented? What practices need to be implemented? Are there other practices not listed that need to be implemented to bring about school turnaround?

3. Imagine you are in charge of conducting the first faculty meeting of the year and your school is launching a turnaround initiative. What would you say to your colleagues in order to generate support for the initiative?

Table 6.1. High-Yield Strategies

High-Yield Strategy	Key Features
Program Review and Alignment	• Evaluation of the match between established content standards and taught curriculum • Evaluation of curriculum in meeting the identified educational needs of students • Evaluation of the effectiveness of instructional strategies • Alignment of curriculum with state assessments
Alignment of Time, People, and Other Resources	• Daily schedules that provide additional learning time in core subjects for struggling students • Maximum use of instructional time • Use of specialized instructional staff within the regular classroom • Advocacy for necessary resources to enhance teaching and learning • Tutoring that supports classroom instruction
Instructionally Focused Teacher Teams	• Staff discusses student achievement data on a regular basis • Staff determines how to assist struggling students
Monitoring of Student Learning	• Staff monitors curriculum content to ensure vertical and horizontal alignment • Regular administration of benchmark assessments to monitor progress in achieving academic targets • Analysis of assessment results by teacher teams • Frequent review and strategic planning in response to assessment results
Targeted Professional Development	• Training focused on specific academic improvement targets identified by teachers • Post-training coaching and monitoring by highly trained experts
Reduction of Behavior Problems and Absenteeism	• Setting of clear behavioral expectations, including attendance • Use of an educative approach with students to teach expectations • Demonstration of respect and caring toward students • Outreach to parents to assist with reinforcement • Celebration of successes • Individualized interventions for students as needed
Family and Community Engagement	• Support for PTO/PTA • Opportunities to create two-way communication between families and the school • Involvement of parents in school-based decision making • Collaboration with community agencies to provide extended services for students

REFERENCES

Deal, Terrence E., and Kent D. Peterson. 1999. *Shaping School Culture: The Heart of Leadership*. San Francisco: Jossey-Bass.

Duke, Daniel L., Pamela D. Tucker, et al. 2005. *Lift-off: Launching the School Turnaround Process in Virginia Schools*. Charlottesville: Partnership for Leaders in Education, University of Virginia.

Elmore, Richard F. 2005. *School Reform from the Inside Out: Policy, Practice, and Performance*. Cambridge, MA: Harvard Education Press.

Epstein, J. L., M. G. Sanders, K. C. Salinas, B. S. Simon, N. R. Jansorn, and F. L. Van Voorhis. 2002. *School, Family, and Community Partnerships: Your Handbook for Action*. 2nd ed. Thousand Oaks, CA: Corwin Press.

Evans, Robert. 1996. *The Human Side of School Change: Reform, Resistance, and the Real-Life Problems of Innovation*. San Francisco: Jossey-Bass.

Goddard, R. D., and L. Skrla. 2006. The Influence of School Social Composition on Teachers' Collective Efficacy Beliefs. *Educational Administration Quarterly* 42(2): 216–35.

Goddard, R. D. 2002. Collective Efficacy and School Organization: A Multilevel Analysis of Teacher Influence in Schools. *Theory and Research in Education Administration* 1: 169–84.

Good, Thomas L., and Jere E. Brophy. 2003. *Looking in Classrooms*. 9th ed. Boston: Allyn & Bacon.

Hall, Gene E., and Shirley M. Hord. 2006. *Implementing Change: Patterns, Principles and Potholes*. Boston: Pearson.

Kennedy, Mary M. 2005. *Inside Teaching: How Classroom Life Undermines Reform*. Cambridge, MA: Harvard University Press.

Kotter, John P. 1996. *Leading Change*. Boston: Harvard Business School Press.

Lortie, Daniel C. 1975. *Schoolteacher: A Sociological Study*. Chicago: University of Chicago Press.

Marzano, Robert J. 2003. *What Works in Schools: Translating Research into Action*. Alexandria, VA: Association for Supervision and Curriculum Development.

Marzano, R. J., T. Waters, and B. A. McNulty. 2005. *School Leadership that Works: From Research to Results*. Alexandria, VA: Association for Supervision and Curriculum Development.

Newmann, F. M., B. Smith, E. Allensworth, and A. S. Bryk. 2001. Instructional Program Coherence: What It Is and Why It Should Guide School Improvement Policy. *Educational Evaluation and Policy Analysis* 23(4): 297–321.

7

Keys to Sustaining a Successful School Turnaround

It happens at the start of each new year. Family members, friends, and colleagues vow to get to the gym more often, quit smoking, or start saving for retirement. It's hard, but by the end of February these acquaintances have shed a few pounds, replaced cigarettes with chewing gum, or begun contributing to a 401(k). Each has turned around some aspect of his or her life successfully. Checking back in June or July, however, we discover that most have fallen back into their old ways of doing things. Sadly, they have failed to sustain the positive changes they initially made.

Schools undergoing turnaround face the same difficulty as individuals in this regard. Changes might be introduced enthusiastically in the fall and implemented throughout the year, and spring test scores rise dramatically as a result. A year or two later, though—under the same leadership and with the same faculty—the school's performance has slipped. Why? This chapter examines the challenges facing schools that have broken out of the cycle of low performance and wish to maintain their progress. Just as the origins of low performance and the process of school turnaround are not the same for every school, there exists no "recipe" for sustaining success. That said, case studies and other research documenting school improvement offer a number of strategies that, when tailored to fit the needs of your school, can help you to do so.

WHO HOLDS THE KEY TO CONTINUED SUCCESS?

Sustainability cannot be realized by focusing solely on one area or group of people within an organization; all components and constituents must be attended to. In schools, there are five groups of stakeholders involved in achieving sustained success: students, parents, teachers, principals, and central office personnel. Each of these groups will be discussed, though we acknowledge that teachers generally have a greater chance of making an impact with the first three groups than the last two.

> *Turnaround Tip:* Sustaining success requires attention to and action from multiple groups of stakeholders.

Students

Finding a new principal, a revamped schedule, and cleaner facilities upon arriving in September can be exciting for students. Likewise, experiencing academic success through new reading and math programs and after-school tutoring can encourage previously struggling students to develop a positive attitude toward school. Once the test scores are in and turnaround is achieved, however, what can be done to continue to motivate students? Mark Keeler, a principal in Rockingham County, Virginia, faced this question after leading his school through a turnaround effort. His answer: encouraging faculty members to "touch the hearts of students," that is, to focus on building personal connections with them (Keeler and Salmonowicz 2006). Attending to the affective component of education may seem like "fluff" compared with analyzing data and aligning curriculum with state standards, but it should not be dismissed. Some educators are fond of portraying standardized tests as "the enemy," an unwanted obstacle that teachers and students must unite to overcome. This may be an effective motivational tool for a while, but how long can students be expected to put forth effort simply to "beat" the test? Feeling responsible to and connected with their teachers are more authentic and appealing sources of motivation. Paula Frazier, another Rockingham County principal who helped her school turn around, fostered this connection through what she termed the "language of learning" (Frazier and Salmonowicz 2006). In an effort to keep students motivated, teachers in her school were asked to focus on the quality of their verbal interactions with students. Providing verbal feedback that was "immediate, sincere, and specific" was a high priority (5).

Celebrating success is another strategy for motivating students. In each of the schools involved in the School Turnaround Specialist Program (STSP), special emphasis is placed on recognizing students' achievements. Exemplary benchmark test scores are acknowledged over the PA during morning announcements, and prizes are given for good attendance. One principal likes to do the Electric Slide with her fifth graders to celebrate when they all pass a test! Reaching the goal of high achievement, however, does not diminish the necessity of celebration. Reminding students of their (or their former classmates') successes can serve as a confidence boost at the outset of a new school year and can create a norm of high achievement.

A more "nuts and bolts" strategy for helping students sustain academic progress is keeping in place the support structures that initially aided them in turning around their performance. Just as chapter 5 mentioned the frustration that can arise among teachers when resources that helped bring about improvement disappear, students can become disheartened if the tutoring or afterschool program that previously provided additional learning opportunities is discontinued.

> *Turnaround Trap:* Reducing resources or eliminating programs that contributed to students' improved performance can undermine efforts to maintain higher achievement.

Finally, increasing the focus on individual students is an important step for sustained success. Whereas a turnaround effort initially may focus broadly on schoolwide issues like aligned curriculum and new curricular programs, continued success depends upon increased specificity and individualization. For example, after taking care of programmatic issues in year one of her principalship, Kim Yates, a turnaround specialist in Danville, Virginia, led her faculty in developing an individualized remediation or enrichment plan for *every one* of the more than two hundred students at her school. Attending to individuals also can be accomplished through differentiated instruction, which takes into account specific students' needs, interests, and strengths while addressing the basic concepts that all students must learn (Tomlinson 1999, 2003).

Parents

Educators, researchers, and parents themselves have debated how and to
what extent parents should be involved in schools. It is clear, however,
that making parents partners in the educational process can be beneficial
to students and schools (Epstein et al. 2002). At the start of a turnaround
initiative, this may not be difficult. Curiosity about a new principal may
draw more parents to the fall open house, and sending benchmark test results home may pique parents' interest in their children's achievement.
But as time goes by, how can parent involvement be maintained and even
increased?

Encouraging parents to participate in your school's PTA or PTO is one
worthwhile way to achieve this goal. The turnaround schools we studied
were creative in this endeavor. One school's meetings were conducted in
community centers near students' homes, while another's meetings were
held in conjunction with school events, like the school's winter concert.
These involved parents can maintain support for your school among other
parents and community members, and may help foster partnerships with
businesses, churches, or other local agencies. They also can help continue
initiatives during times of transition. When the principal who leads a school
turnaround effort leaves, for example, parents involved with the PTA or
PTO can work with teachers to strongly advocate for the school's needs
while the new principal builds political capital with the superintendent and
school board. As one turnaround specialist explained during a training ses-
sion, "The parents need to know how to ask for things once I'm gone."

Teachers

Nearly every week during the winter months, the following scenario plays
out in a college basketball arena somewhere in the United States. The fans
are going crazy. Their team, losing by fifteen points with eight minutes to
go, somehow has managed to make a comeback and tie the score. In overtime, though, the opposing squad scores ten quick points and the home
team ends up losing the game. While leaving the arena, the casual observer wonders why the home team, which seemed to have all the momentum, suddenly collapsed. The experienced fan, however, knows what
just happened: The home team "ran out of gas." The players put all of

their energy into eliminating their deficit and were unable to maintain the same level of energy in overtime. It would not be unexpected for teachers who are a part of a successful turnaround effort to face a similar situation, since tremendous commitment and energy from faculty members is necessary to improve student achievement. So how can a possible postturnaround burnout letdown be avoided?

One possibility is to "work smarter, not harder," by increasing collaboration with colleagues. A veteran kindergarten teacher at a school involved in the STSP described the way his grade-level team collaborates: "One thing I love is that not all six of us have to create lesson plans. We can create one lesson plan and follow it . . . as opposed to six different people doing six different things." Two fifth-grade teachers at a different STSP school combined their small classes into one room so that one person could lead the lesson while the other gave support to individual students. One of the teachers remarked, "We've just started, and I already feel a difference in my energy level."

Research has shown that a good portion of the responsibility for reducing teacher burnout belongs to principals. Farber (1991) reviewed a number of studies on teacher stress and burnout and compiled the researchers' suggestions for how principals can best "take care of" their teachers. These included the following:

- Increasing both written and oral communication to teachers
- Providing recognition for good effort and support for what is currently working
- Following up on requests with action, feedback, and more action
- Protecting teachers from impossible demands from parents, politicians, or the school board
- Developing a teacher assistance team
- Offering teachers changes in their routines (teaching a different grade or area; team teaching)
- Offering release time for the development of innovative projects (302–3)

If you get involved in the school turnaround process and begin to see signs of fatigue and burnout in yourself or fellow teachers, it may be a good idea to suggest to your principal ways in which he or she can help.

Another way for you and your colleagues to conserve energy (as well as time and resources) is to prevent expertise from leaving your school. As you undoubtedly have seen, when good teachers retire or transfer to another district, their "trade secrets" often leave with them. Not only are their ideas and advice no longer present in committee and grade-level meetings, but the novice teachers who often take their place may not have enough experience to contribute their own best practices to discussions. Fortunately, it is possible to minimize the effects of losing a talented faculty member. In a recent government report from England that addressed poorly performing schools that recovered and sustained success, debriefing key faculty members who planned to leave was offered as a strategy to "help other people carry on the good work" (National Audit Office 2006, 51). Conducting this sort of exit interview can allow team members to learn from a departing teacher's experience and insights. The report also suggested increasing shadowing of and mentoring by key members of the faculty before they depart.

> *Turnaround Tip:* Interview key faculty members before they leave so that their expertise can continue to assist teachers.

Teachers also can sustain success by refining their practice. However, when professional and staff development activities are offered—professional development referring to individual teachers and staff development referring to groups of teachers (Duke 1987, 126)—they should be targeted to specific areas of need. Staff development, therefore, could address topics such as data analysis and remediation strategies. Professional development, on the other hand, could be aimed at filling skill gaps; a novice fourth-grade teacher might attend a workshop on classroom management while a veteran first-grade teacher learns to use a computer program that assists children with reading difficulties. To get the most out of staff and professional development activities, teachers may want to participate in peer coaching. An "integral part of the professional lives of professionals" in fields like medicine, law, business, and politics, good peer coaching entails working collaboratively with a colleague to give and receive honest feedback about one's practice, with the goal of improving classroom performance (Burbach and Sayeski 2007).

Although turnaround efforts often begin with a new or refocused leader, they cannot be sustained without teachers taking on more leadership roles.

The first step in this process is the principal's willingness to distribute leadership. Presuming this happens, teachers must be equally willing to accept the added responsibility, which may include making school policy decisions, implementing new programs, and selecting professional development activities (Chrisman 2005). When teachers assume increased leadership, a school's goals and strategies are more likely to reflect faculty members' beliefs and talents as well as to enjoy schoolwide support. In a 2006 study, Muijs and Harris found that teacher leadership helped to harness teacher creativity, empower teachers and motivate them to improve performance, and increase the chances of teacher retention and the effectiveness of teacher recruitment. Additionally, the presence of teacher leadership means success is not dependent upon an exceptional administrator and can be sustained when that person leaves (National Audit Office 2006).

Principals

Training for school administrators typically revolves around how to identify and solve problems, which is helpful when it comes to turning around a school. Sustaining success can be challenging for principals, however, because doing so requires them to readjust their focus from problem-solving to something they usually have not been prepared to do: fine-tune what is going well. Disciplined record-keeping is a simple first step that can help principals move in this direction. An inventory of successful programs and changes, as well as teachers' successes with individual students, can serve as a starting point for discussions with the faculty about making adjustments where needed.

Another area in which principals generally do not receive training is leadership succession. Because school leaders have little or no say over who replaces them, the most valuable course a leader can take to prepare for his or her eventual departure is to distribute leadership to teachers. Sara Jamison, whose story you have been following throughout the book, put this principle into practice with a nudge from her teachers:

> In a reading curriculum program we started in the summer after the first year, I put the reading teachers together and set up a meeting structure. By the third meeting the faculty members involved said very nicely, "Don't you have something to do in that office? Can't you go do something?" I took

that as a good thing. I needed to step out and be quiet. They recognized that when they harnessed the strength of each other, they could work with a really difficult population and be successful. That's what's going to sustain them in the long run.

Principals also can maintain a school's success through their personnel decisions. In all but one of the nineteen schools involved in the first two cohorts of the School Turnaround Specialist Program, principals perceived personnel problems to be an obstacle to overcoming low performance (Duke et al. 2007). Dismissing someone who is ineffective may be required during a turnaround, but that action must be followed by hiring someone who will fit in with the existing team of teachers and the school culture. One way to find the right person is to widen the scope of the search. J. Harrison-Coleman, a turnaround specialist in Portsmouth, Virginia, used the Internet to widen her search for candidates that would be a good match for her school. The search resulted in her hiring teachers from three states west of the Mississippi River: Arizona, North Dakota, and Washington. Soliciting key faculty members (department chairs, team leaders, etc.) to conduct a group interview with a prospective teacher is another method to ensure a good fit. When new teachers are hired, of course, mentoring and other supports will be needed to integrate them into the faculty and promote their professional growth.

Central Office

In the same study of the nineteen turnaround schools that was mentioned in the previous section, Duke and colleagues (2007) found that only four of the principals perceived lack of support from the central office as being a problem. This makes sense considering that low-performing schools often get plenty of resources and support from their districts in order to improve. The danger lies in prematurely reducing resources and support once turnaround is achieved. Central office personnel should recognize that it may take years of extra assistance — such as classroom observations by district specialists and increased funding to continue supplementary programs and recruit talented teachers — once turnaround is achieved before a school can "fly on its own." And if it appears that the central office does not recognize this need, teachers need to advocate for continued support.

Another matter for the central office to consider is leadership succession, as picking the right principal to lead following a turnaround will affect significantly a school's ability to build on its newfound success. We can look to the NBA to observe the impact of such a choice. Phil Jackson, current head coach of the NBA's Los Angeles Lakers, was hired by two franchises—the Chicago Bulls in the late 1980s and the Lakers in the late 1990s—that were successful before his appointment but unable to win a championship. In both cases, Jackson took the same complement of gifted players that the previous coach had and won multiple championships. Critics claim that Jackson would be unable to win a championship if placed in a situation where he had to rebuild, or turn around, a team. Implicit in that criticism, however, is the assumption that a single leader should be able to guide an organization all the way from low performance to truly exceptional performance. It may be that one type of leader is well-suited to lead a turnaround effort, while another type of leader possesses the skill set needed to sustain success, and yet another is required to help the organization make the leap to greatness. Those in the central office who are responsible for hiring school administrators should consider during their recruitment and interview processes the "type" of leader needed after a successful turnaround. Just as important, faculty members should reflect on this issue and communicate their thoughts to the central office during the early stages of the hiring process.

STAYING ON COURSE

Becoming successful is hard, but holding onto success once it is attained is even harder. This is especially so in schools, where so many opportunities for backsliding exist. Changing student demographics, failure to properly analyze data trends, faculty resistance to change, and complacency in the school, district, and community all can be threats to continued high achievement (see Salmonowicz, in press, for an illustrative case study). Similar to rock climbing, where "protection" devices are placed in the rock to prevent falling below the last chunk of progress made, educators at a turned-around school must hold the current level of achievement steady while simultaneously working to improve it. Following are some processes that can help you and your school undertake this challenging work.

Self-Evaluation

Britain's National Audit Office noted that, of the various factors involved in sustaining success in schools, "a culture of self-evaluation and improvement is key" (2006, 50). Such a culture is vital for both individual teachers and administrators and larger entities like grade-level teams, school committees, and academic programs. After all, it is crucial to know whether or not the personnel and programmatic changes begun during turnaround truly are working! In *Built to Last*, Collins and Porras address the continuous improvement that defines visionary companies, explaining that these organizations "install powerful mechanisms to create *dis*comfort—to obliterate complacency—and thereby stimulate change and improvement *before* the external world demands it" (1994, 187).

> *Turnaround Tip:* Continuously evaluate existing programs and practices to make certain they are effective.

> *Turnaround Trap:* A school environment that feels comfortable and lacks tension can hinder efforts to engage in self-evaluation and make improvements.

Whereas turning around a school requires you and your school to make major changes, engaging in self-evaluation and improvement efforts should result in small adjustments to the things you already are doing. In 2002, after turning around her school to the point where its test scores in nearly every grade and subject were higher than both the district and state averages, principal Paula Frazier still pushed for minor improvements. She led her teachers in digging deeper into the achievement data than they had in the past, adjusting the third-grade schedule to allow more time for reading and language arts, and providing students with testing strategies to boost their confidence and performance during state tests in the spring (Frazier and Salmonowicz 2006). Sara Jamison explains the process of continuous improvement like this: "It's been more subtle changes along the way. It hasn't been the dramatic kind of shifts in course like we had during the first year. It's just a cycle that keeps spiraling and spiraling, picking up some things and then going up, then taking a new form and going up again."

Institutionalizing the Culture

It is important to note that the National Audit Office report cited earlier did not say simply that self-evaluation and improvement are needed to sustain success; it said that a *culture* of self-evaluation and improvement is key. As DuFour and Eaker point out, "Until changes become so entrenched that they represent part of 'the way we do things around here,' they are extremely fragile and subject to regression" (1998, 105). But how is it possible for your school to become a place where a culture of best practices in teaching, collaboration and teamwork, focused professional development, and self-evaluation and improvement is institutionalized?

Deal and Peterson (1999) suggest the following ways, among others, in which school leaders (including administrators, faculty, staff, and parents) can shape school culture:

- Strengthen elements of the existing culture that are positive and supportive of core values.
- Build on the established traditions and values, adding new, constructive ones to the existing combination.
- Recruit, hire, and socialize staff who share the values of the culture and who will add new insights or skills to the culture.
- Sustain core norms, values, and beliefs in everything the school does. (115–16)

No two school cultures are exactly the same, but those that are successful tend to exhibit common characteristics. These include a shared sense of respect and caring, positive beliefs about students' potential, shared leadership, a focus on student and teacher learning, and a professional community committed to improving practice (Deal and Peterson 1999, 116). It is important for you and your colleagues to recognize the positive elements of your school's culture, as well as how they came to be, so the culture can be preserved.

REACHING A STATE OF SUSTAINED SUCCESS

The transition from school turnaround to sustained success can be difficult. Jim Collins labels this part of organizational improvement "the flywheel."

At first, as teachers often witness during the turnaround process, the wheel (i.e., change efforts) moves slowly. Rotating it just one time takes a lot of effort. In time, though, the wheel begins to move with less effort:

> Then, at some point—breakthrough! The momentum of the thing kicks in in your favor, hurling the flywheel forward, turn after turn . . . whoosh! . . . its own heavy weight working for you. . . . Each turn of the flywheel builds upon work done earlier, compounding your investment of effort. A thousand times faster, then ten thousand, then a hundred thousand. The huge heavy disk flies forward, with almost unstoppable momentum. (Collins 2001, 164–65)

We hope you are encouraged and excited about the prospects of turning around your school and gathering this type of momentum toward sustained success. But what about colleagues who continue to resist the changes that will need to take place for this to happen? That is one of the topics addressed in the next chapter, which focuses on the change process itself.

FOLLOW-UP ACTIVITIES

1. Create a list of ten questions you would ask a respected colleague about his or her experiences as a teacher if that person were planning to leave your school. Next, meet with a teacher at your school or another school and conduct a "dry run" to ensure the questions are clear to the interviewee and draw out the useful insights you are looking for. Afterward, refine your questions so they are ready whenever you need them.
2. Spend a day at a consistently high-performing school, either by yourself or with colleagues from your school. Observe classrooms and talk with teachers (and, if possible, administrators). Ask them what they have done to sustain success, individually and schoolwide. Share the results of your visit at a faculty meeting and make concrete recommendations about what ideas your school could consider for adoption.
3. Once your school has turned around, do your part to ensure that formal discussions about sustaining success begin. Make it an agenda

item with the committees and teams of which you are a member, and suggest to your principal that this topic be made the focal point of at least one faculty meeting.

REFERENCES

Burbach, H. J., and B. Sayeski. 2007. A Peer Coaching Model for Improving the Instructional and Organizational Learning Capacity of Your School (Web Exclusive). *Principal* 86(3).

Chrisman, V. 2005. How Schools Sustain Success. *Educational Leadership* 62(5): 16–20.

Collins, J. 2001. *Good to Great.* New York: HarperCollins.

Collins, J., and J. I. Porras. 1994. *Built to Last.* New York: HarperCollins.

Deal, T. E., and K. D. Peterson. 1999. *Shaping School Culture.* San Francisco: Jossey-Bass.

DuFour, R., and R. Eaker. 1998. *Professional Learning Communities at Work.* Bloomington, IN: National Education Service.

Duke, D. L. 1987. *School Leadership and Instructional Improvement.* New York: Random House.

Duke, D. L., P. D. Tucker, M. J. Salmonowicz, and M. K. Levy. 2007. How Comparable Are the Perceived Challenges Facing Principals of Low-Performing Schools? *International Studies in Educational Administration* 35(1): 3–21.

Epstein, J. L., M. G. Sanders, K. C. Salinas, B. S. Simon, N. R. Jansorn, and F. L. Van Voorhis. 2002. *School, Family, and Community Partnerships: Your Handbook for Action.* 2nd ed. Thousand Oaks, CA: Corwin Press.

Farber, B. A. 1991. *Crisis in Education.* San Francisco: Jossey-Bass.

Frazier, P., and M. J. Salmonowicz. 2006. *Pleasant Valley Elementary School: Celebrating Success One Student at a Time* (UVA-OB-0882). Charlottesville, VA: Darden Business Publishing.

Keeler, M., and M. J. Salmonowicz. 2006. *South River Elementary School: Touching the Hearts and Minds of Students* (UVA-OB-0883). Charlottesville, VA: Darden Business Publishing.

Muijs, D., and A. Harris. 2006. Teacher Led School Improvement: Teacher Leadership in the UK. *Teacher and Teacher Education* 22: 961–72.

National Audit Office, Department for Education and Skills. 2006. *Improving Poorly Performing Schools in England.* London: Author.

Salmonowicz, M. J. In press. Scott O'Neill and Lincoln Elementary School: Preventing a Slide from Good to Worse. *Journal of Cases in Educational Leadership.*

Tomlinson, C. A. 1999. *The Differentiated Classroom: Responding to the Needs of All Learners*. Alexandria, VA: Association for Supervision and Curriculum Development.

———. 2003. *Fulfilling the Promise of the Differentiated Classroom: Strategies and Tools for Responsive Teaching*. Alexandria, VA: Association for Supervision and Curriculum Development.

8

Those Who Can, Teach;
Those Who Can Teach, Change

Let's face it, to be a professional educator in these times of ever-shifting state and federal policies, economic ups and downs, population changes, and ever-rising expectations requires considerable flexibility and adaptability. In a word, change. People say that the only constant is change. But people also say that the more things change, the more they remain the same. These two seemingly antithetical expressions capture our ambivalence about change. Change is typically regarded as necessary—for others. We want parents to be better parents, students to be more diligent students, administrators to be more supportive administrators, taxpayers to be more generous taxpayers, and so on. But what about us? When the need to change stares us in the face, we often feel like diverting our eyes. As adults, teachers lead lives characterized by complexity and multiple demands. It is not surprising that the need for change may be greeted with little enthusiasm. The theme that echoes throughout this book, however, is loud and clear—low-performing schools will not improve unless and until those who work in them embrace change.

Admonition is in order. Don't confuse a change in status with professional growth. Just because we switch grade levels or teach a new subject or are chosen for a leadership role does not mean that we have changed in any substantive way. We may perform in our new circumstances the same way we did previously. All that's really changed is our assignment. Professional growth, on the other hand, requires the acquisition and application of new skills, new understandings, and new beliefs.

In this chapter, we take an "up close and personal" look at the change process and how it can impact you and your colleagues. We do so because we believe in the old saying, "Forewarned is forearmed." The professional growth needed to turn around a low-performing school demands considerable energy and resolve. Understanding as much as you can about how individuals change is good preparation for the rigors of school improvement.

The chapter opens with a discussion of the change process as it unfolds in schools and its implications for individual organization members. The next section addresses some of the signs that the school turnaround process is not going well. If every teacher becomes a troubleshooter and recognizes these signs, perhaps the problems that invariably arise during school improvement can be identified early and handled before they undermine the entire process. One major problem, of course, is resistance to change. The following section examines several reasons why some teachers may resist school improvement efforts. The chapter closes with a review of several important personal attributes that are associated with a positive response to change.

SCHOOL TURNAROUND IS A PROCESS

To the casual observer, a school turnaround may appear to be an event. Last year Greenfield Elementary School was a locus of low performance; this year it is a citadel of academic success. In reality, of course, there are no overnight miracles. Improving a low-performing school is a process, one that may take several years. Students of organizational change have characterized the process as consisting of various stages.

A simple model of the change process consists of three stages: initiation, implementation, and incorporation. The process begins when someone or some group initiates a call for change. This step is followed by the implementation of something new—a program, policy, practice, or other reform. When the "something new" has been fully accepted, the change is said to be incorporated into the day-to-day operations of the organization.

After reviewing various models of the change process, Duke (2004, 29) opted for a four-stage model: discovery, design, development, and implementation. During the initial, or discovery, stage of change, people must decide whether or not there is a need for change. If a need is found, they probably will have to come up with a justification for change that will be acceptable to key stakeholders.

Imagine that for several years a high school has recorded low scores on state tests in mathematics. The math teachers meet with school administrators and decide that a change in the school schedule is needed in order to provide struggling students with additional time during the school day to receive instruction and assistance. The proposal is presented to the rest of the high school faculty in the hopes that they will support the need for change. Teachers of other subjects are sympathetic, but some teachers are concerned that an increase in time for math might cut into time and enrollments for their own classes. Several teachers, including teachers of foreign languages, make it clear that they like the forty-five-minute periods in the existing schedule.

These concerns must be addressed during the second, or design, stage of the change process. This is when teachers, administrators, and perhaps outside consultants attempt to create a daily schedule that allows math teachers to spend an extended period of time with certain students without interfering with the preferred arrangements of other teachers. One option—a standard block schedule in which class periods are doubled in length and courses meet every other day—is ruled out because some teachers want to maintain daily forty-five-minute periods. Eventually a schedule is designed that provides two ninety-minute blocks each day for teachers who desire more time to work with students. Math classes are scheduled during these times. The remainder of the school day is scheduled for standard forty-five-minute periods.

Once a schedule design has been accepted, a plan for putting the new schedule into place needs to be developed. During this development stage of the change process, planners anticipate what will be required to achieve as smooth a change as possible. Parents and students, of course, will have to be informed. Administrators and guidance counselors will need to determine how the shift to a new schedule will impact the course options available to students. A process must be worked out for assigning low-performing math students to double-block math classes. Teachers of double-block classes will require staff development training on how to organize ninety-minute classes so that students maintain a high level of engagement.

Having anticipated what is needed to implement the new schedule, the high school is ready for the fourth stage of the change process— implementation. Implementation invariably leads to unanticipated challenges that can send planners back to the drawing board. Fortunately, the planners in the present case expected unforeseen problems and designated a pilot year in which to work out the kinks in the new schedule. At the end of the first year of implementation, the faculty will meet and identify all of the concerns that must be resolved in order for the schedule to achieve its intended purpose without damaging other elements of the school program.

Stage models can be helpful in informing educators about the components of the change process that need to be addressed in order to turn around a low-performing school. It should be noted, however, that change rarely unfolds in a neat and linear fashion. Stages sometime overlap, and they do not always occur in the prescribed sequence. Sometimes, for example, individuals latch on to a design before they have discovered a need for change to justify its adoption. In other cases, planning may be ongoing, extending well into the implementation of a reform. There is no telling how people who were supportive of the need for change will react once they are faced with the actual implementation of a reform. Few people seem to be able to anticipate just how much time, energy, and emotional adjustment will be required to achieve meaningful change.

A Change Is Not a Transition

To help reformers appreciate the impact of organizational change on the lives of individuals, William Bridges (2003) developed a unique model of the change process. His focus is not on the organization, but on the individuals who are expected to carry out the process of change. He distinguishes between changes and transitions. Changes are situational; transitions are psychological. With a change, the focus is on the desired outcome and how to achieve it. With a transition, attention is directed to what will be left behind when the change occurs. Transitions, in other words, begin with a sense of loss.

Bridges maintains that there are three stages to transition: (1) ending, (2) the neutral zone, and (3) a new beginning. He makes the case that changes without transitions are unlikely to be very successful. What he means is that individuals must make a psychological adjustment to change if the change is to accomplish what it is intended to accomplish.

> *Turnaround Tip:* Successful change requires a psychological transition. The first stage of this transition involves acknowledging a sense of loss regarding what is to be changed.

Transition begins when people recognize what they must let go of in order for change to occur. It may seem odd that teachers would experience a sense of loss when confronted with the need to improve a low-performing school, but such is likely to be the case. No matter how bad a situation, it has the benefit of being familiar. Veteran teachers develop relationships and routines over the years. A school turnaround initiative can threaten to disrupt these relationships and upset long-established routines. It is wise to expect a certain degree of separation anxiety and loss when embarking on a course of significant school improvement.

The second stage is referred to as the "neutral zone." Bridges explains that individuals engaged in the change process reach a point where they finally have bid good-bye to their old circumstances, but they are as yet unclear about where they are headed. When people enter the neutral zone, they are apt to feel overloaded and adrift. Priorities are uncertain, and people feel disoriented. Among the symptoms of the neutral zone are increased absenteeism and divisions among staff members. Some people want to rush forward while others yearn for the old days.

Assuming people are patient and willing to deal with the ambiguities of the neutral zone, they eventually reach the "new beginning" stage of the transition process. At this point, they start to identify with the intended change. With this identification comes new energy and a clear sense of purpose. People recognize why it was so necessary to abandon the previous situation and move on to something better. Resistance to change diminishes.

The great value of Bridges's model of the transition process is that it captures the stresses and strains that individuals must handle as they experience organizational change. Being prepared for these "by-products" of change can be of great benefit to those committed to improving low-performing schools.

The Experience of Change Varies

Despite the emphasis on teamwork and collaboration in the previous chapters, when it comes to organizational change, teachers first experience the process as individuals. If we consider the model developed by Bridges, this means that some teachers will have reached a new beginning while their colleagues are still dealing with the neutral zone or the ending stage. It is reasonable, of course, to want all the members of a faculty eventually to wind up at the same destination, but it is unreasonable to think that they will all get there having traveled identical routes.

The notion that people undergo the change process in idiosyncratic ways is reinforced by the work of Frances Fuller and Gene Hall. Fuller (1970) studied the concerns of student teachers and experienced teachers. She discovered that concerns tend to evolve with experience. Preservice teachers initially were concerned about matters that had little to do with teaching. Once student teachers began their supervised teaching and had direct contact with students, their concerns began to focus on egocentric issues. They worried about whether they would be accepted by veteran teachers and whether they would succeed at teaching. They even worried about whether they could find a parking place at their assigned school!

As student teaching progressed, concerns shifted from *self* to *tasks*. Student teachers wondered how they would get all their papers graded when they were exhausted after a day's work. They worried about how they could manage different groups of students as they worked on in-class assignments. Concern for *impact*—making a difference in the learning and lives of students—characterized experienced teachers far more than student teachers. Presumably the experienced teachers already had addressed self and task concerns reasonably well and thus were free to focus on the welfare of their students.

Based on Fuller's findings, Gene Hall and Shirlye Hord (2001) at the University of Texas developed a model called Stages of Concern. Consisting of seven levels, Stages of Concern can be used to identify where individual teachers are in terms of their interest in a particular reform or change. Let's say the change was a school turnaround initiative at a low-performing school. At the first level, referred to as "awareness," teachers are not concerned at all about school turnaround. When teachers want to know more about the school turnaround process in general, they have reached the second or informational stage of concern. Teachers who begin to wonder how the school turnaround process will affect them personally are at the third or personal stage of concern. The first three stages correspond to Fuller's two initial concerns—unrelated and self concerns.

Teachers who become involved in the school turnaround process and encounter some challenges regarding how to do what is expected of them have reached the management stage, representing Fuller's task concerns. Assuming teachers are able to address these concerns effectively, they move on to concerns about impact. The first stage of concern about impact involves consequences. Teachers focus on how the school turnaround process is affecting their students. The next stage of concern—collaboration—entails linking together the efforts of all faculty members. The focus, in other words, is on coordinating one's own school turnaround efforts with those of one's fellow teachers. Refocusing—the final stage of concern—finds teachers exploring ways to improve upon the original school turnaround process. By this point, they know what is and is not working well, and they care enough about the school turnaround process to want to make it as productive as possible.

The works of Fuller and Hall remind us that individuals respond to change idiosyncratically. It is naïve to expect a first-year teacher to share exactly the same concerns as a seasoned veteran. School administrators and experienced teachers must take the lead in assisting new teachers in addressing lower-level concerns so that they eventually can focus on impact concerns. Successful school turnaround initiatives require an understanding of how different teachers deal with the change process.

> *Turnaround Trap:* Expecting all teachers to react similarly to the changes associated with turning around a low-performing school is unrealistic.

TROUBLESHOOTING THE TURNAROUND PROCESS

Raising student achievement in a low-performing school can be a tall order for even the most competent teachers. Nothing short of comprehensive, systemic change will suffice. Writing about change, University of Washington researchers (Knapp et al. 1998, 404) state,

> These reforms typically call for fundamental changes in teachers' thinking about learning, the subject matter they teach, and the ways they engage

learners in this subject matter, not to mention the way they interact with each other in the collegial "community" of the school. Accordingly, the reforms bring new demands, often experienced by teachers as burdens.

Given the sweeping nature of changes entailed in a school turnaround, it is unwise to expect the process to unfold effortlessly and to be free of problems. If you become involved in a school turnaround project, what obstacles might you expect to encounter?

One way to troubleshoot school turnarounds is to focus on each stage of the change process. Earlier in this chapter, a four-stage model of change was described. The stages were labeled discovery, design, development, and implementation. Let us consider what might go wrong at each stage.

During the discovery stage of the school turnaround process, teachers and administrators engage in pinpointing the deficiencies in school organization, programs, policies, and practices that need to be addressed in order to raise student achievement. One problem that can arise involves the overidentification of areas in need of change. School personnel become overwhelmed when the need for change is so extensive that it seems beyond their capacity. They are more likely to embrace the school turnaround process if they can focus on a limited set of changes.

Another problem may involve misdiagnosing the causes of student learning deficits. Attributing deficits to symptoms instead of root causes can result in inappropriate strategies for raising student achievement. Consider once again a school with low math achievement. Faculty members may determine that the problem is the result of students not knowing all of the math standards. A proposal is made to double the time students spend in math classes. When the proposal is implemented, no improvement in math scores occurs. Math scores, in fact, continue to fall. The real source of low math achievement turns out to be inadequate instructional practices on the part of the math teachers. Doubling the amount of instruction when the instruction is inadequate to begin with is not a solution. It simply compounds the problem.

One of the most serious problems that can arise during the discovery stage of change concerns the failure to involve key stakeholders in diagnosing the need for change. Key stakeholders include school faculty and staff, parents, and students. Each group is likely to have a different perspective on what is required for the school turnaround process. While it may be impossible to accommodate everyone's views, all parties deserve to have a voice in the process. Failure to listen to diverse views at the outset of change may subsequently result in a lack of broad-based support for turnaround efforts.

The second stage of the change process involved the adoption, adaptation, or creation of a design for change. The design is likely to encompass a variety of elements, ranging from curriculum alignment to benchmark testing to new interventions for low achievers. One risk associated with the design stage concerns the failure of teachers and administrators to consider a wide range of design options. Choosing to adopt the first reading program that designers encounter, for example, is unwise. A systematic review of a variety of programs always should precede the choice of a particular program. Data needs to be gathered, for example, on how previous adopters evaluated their reading programs. While time-consuming, a thorough examination of alternatives usually pays dividends in the long run. Considerable time and money can be wasted by making a hasty—and ultimately incorrect—choice.

Another design problem involves a poor match between the need for change and the change itself. Adopting a highly scripted and comprehensive reading program when test data indicate that students are struggling only in spelling and vocabulary may not make much sense. A supplementary program targeting these two areas of literacy may be a wiser choice.

Every design for school improvement has the potential to produce negative side effects. It is important for teachers and administrators engaged in the school turnaround process to anticipate possible side effects and decide whether to proceed anyway. A design that relies on extensive homework assignments to raise achievement may seem like a useful change, but it runs the risk of cutting into family time. It also can place certain students whose parents are unable or unwilling to assist with homework at a decided disadvantage. Knowing of these possible negative side effects in advance, teachers can arrange for a homework assistance period during lunch or immediately after school.

Turnaround Tip: No matter what the proposed change, teachers should anticipate possible negative side effects and decide whether they merit adjustments in the proposed change.

The third stage of the change process—the development stage—involves planning for the implementation of change. Here, too, problems can arise.

We already have noted that teachers are likely to find themselves at various levels of readiness for change. Some teachers may be anxious to get started on a school turnaround initiative while others are reluctant to admit that any change is necessary. Given these variations, it is important that the entire faculty share a common understanding of the plans for school turnaround. In particular, every teacher should be clear about his or her own role in the change process. And make no mistake—every teacher needs to have a role in the change process. When school improvement plans include only a select number of faculty members, they can result in divisiveness and hurt feelings.

Teachers are not the only ones who need to be informed about plans for change. During the development stage, parents and other community members should have opportunities to learn about what will be entailed in efforts to raise student achievement and to offer their own suggestions. This is a good time to solicit volunteers and develop partnerships with local businesses and other organizations. When people feel left out of the preliminary stages of the change process, they are less likely to support the changes once they are implemented.

Resources to support the change process must be secured during the development stage. When planners fail to anticipate resource needs accurately and when they only plan for the near future, they may be sowing the seeds of subsequent problems. Consider staff development. School turnaround initiatives certainly require in-service training to get started on a new course, but the need for training does not disappear when the turnaround process commences. Staff development must be ongoing and provide for bringing newly hired teachers up to speed. Planners therefore need to make sure that resources are available to support sustained staff development. The history of educational reform is littered with examples of reforms that stalled because resources only were secured for the first year of the change process.

> *Turnaround Trap:* Building a one-year budget to support changes that
> are likely to take several years to implement can lead to a loss of mo-
> mentum when a school is unable to secure additional resources.

Once a need for change has been identified, a design for change has been chosen, and a plan for change has been developed, the time has come for implementation of change to begin. Teachers and administrators once again must be on the alert for trouble. Problems can occur when people are confused about their role in the change process. Sometimes this confusion is not due to poor planning, but to new mandates that impact a school *after* the school turnaround process has begun (Knapp et al. 1998). Teachers thought they were clear about what they needed to do to implement a turnaround plan, but then the school board or a government agency announces a new policy or program that requires teachers to assume new responsibilities. The world, after all, does not stop because a school embarks on an improvement plan. It is important to reconsider responsibilities in light of any changes that occur after implementation of a turnaround plan has begun. Never take for granted that people are clear about how to balance new commitments and prior commitments.

Students of organizational change have identified two potential sources of problems during the implementation stage. The first involves premature celebration, or what Kanter (2004) refers to as a "false positive." As a result of enormous effort, enthusiasm, and focused energy, a school can achieve some pretty impressive achievement gains in a relatively short time period. While acknowledging this accomplishment is understandable, teachers should be cautious about declaring the turnaround completed at this point. A one-time boost in test scores does not constitute school turnaround. If teachers ease up after the receipt of the first set of encouraging test scores, the likelihood is great that success will not be sustained.

Turnaround Trap: Beware of celebrating early successes. It can lead to premature complacency and loss of momentum.

Another pothole in the road to school improvement is the mirror opposite of premature celebration. Fullan (2001, 40) refers to this phenomenon as the "implementation dip." In his examination of research on organizational change, he has found that things often get worse before they get better. Immediately after launching a whole battery of changes in order to effect a school turnaround, it would not be unusual, for example, for student achievement and faculty morale to falter. Change typically is accompanied by uncertainty, and uncertainty can lead to performance problems. It is crucial, therefore, that teachers resist the temptation to declare the battle lost just because the initial results of implementation are disappointing.

Sometimes a sign of trouble during implementation involves what does not happen. When people stop discussing their concerns, the change process is at risk. The reason is obvious. It is impossible to address implementation problems if people refrain from sharing them. Why would teachers stop discussing their concerns? They could be disheartened or angry that previous expressions or concern did not result in any constructive corrective action. Or they could be feeling tired and isolated. Whatever the reason, a reduction in communication between and among members of the school community is almost always a sign of trouble. School improvement thrives on open, honest, and ongoing discussion.

We have seen some examples of organizational problems that can arise at various points on the journey to school turnaround. It also is possible that individuals will find reasons to resist the process at each step along the way. The next section explores some of these reasons.

WHY DO SOME TEACHERS RESIST CHANGE?

That people resist change should come as no surprise. In some cases resistance is understandable and reasonable. In other cases resistance seems arbitrary or self-serving. When thinking about resistance to change, it is crucial to bear one point in mind: A low-performing school cannot improve unless and until the professionals in that school embrace change. And improve these schools must if the children they serve are to have a reasonable chance to succeed in life.

Whether teachers embrace or resist the changes accompanying the school turnaround process can be a function of many factors, including their age, stage of career, physical health, mental health, training, upbringing, beliefs, and experience. A special education teacher, for example, may look at low-achieving, unmotivated students differently from a teacher of Advanced Placement courses. Faced with challenging students, the Advanced Placement teacher feels inadequate, an uncomfortable feeling for a professional educator. The special education teacher, on the other hand, possesses the confidence to confront the students and help them to learn. Her confidence derives from her training in strategies for assisting struggling students.

In this section we examine some of the reasons why individual teachers may resist school improvement efforts. The reasons are related to risk of failure, disillusionment, inconvenience, increased work, impact on personal life, and the possible threat to job security (Duke 2004, 124–29; Knapp et al. 1998). While there are certainly additional reasons for resistance, a discussion of these reasons should provide some sense of the hurdles that may have to be cleared in order to get all members of a faculty moving forward.

Risk of Failure

No one likes to fail, but it is not fear of failure that causes many people to resist change. It is fear of the imagined consequences of failure. Failing is associated with loss of respect and admiration. Fear of losing the respect and admiration of colleagues and clients can lead certain individuals to confront change cautiously. Change, especially an ambitious change like turning around a low-performing school, is never a sure thing. The potential for failure is ever present. The cautious teacher who fears the imagined consequences of trying and failing at improving his teaching may not even realize that continuing to teach in a low-performing school is itself a form of failure. The only true failure is failure to try to improve an unacceptable educational situation.

Disillusionment

School improvement initiatives are nothing new for many veteran teachers, especially those who work in low-performing schools. They have seen reforms come and go. Often the arrival of a new superintendent or principal is accompanied by a variety of changes. When teachers invest considerable time, energy, and hope in a set of reforms only to see the reforms abandoned when a new leader arrives, they can become understandably skeptical and disillusioned. As a consequence, they are more likely to resist subsequent school improvement efforts.

Inconvenience

New teachers are encouraged to develop routines for dealing with predictable classroom situations. Skilled teachers have dozens of routines for handling everything from correcting inappropriate behavior to distributing instructional materials. Over the years teachers become so comfortable with their routines that they often are unaware of them. The routines have become second nature. Anytime changes are proposed as part of some school improvement initiative, the potential exists for disrupting these routines. The prospect of teachers having to leave their "comfort zone" and try new ways of doing things can be disconcerting and may result in resistance to change. It is important for teachers to realize that routines which once were useful may no longer be effective. The only way to tell whether a routine is still effective is to break the routine for a period of time and try something different.

Increased Work

There is no way around the fact that turning around a low-performing school involves an increased workload for teachers. Meetings must be convened to identify problems, design corrective strategies, and plan for school improvement. Once reforms are in place, meetings do not cease, however. That is because continued teacher collaboration is a key ingredient in the school turnaround process. Raising student achievement is contingent on teachers working in teams to analyze data on student progress, align curriculum and instruction, and deliver assistance to struggling students. Additional time is required for ongoing staff development. When teachers already were feeling overwhelmed prior to a school turnaround initiative, the prospect of even more work may be discouraging. The experience of successful school turnaround projects has shown, however, that most teachers eventually come to appreciate the opportunity to collaborate with their colleagues, even if it does entail more work.

Impact on Personal Life

The increased workload associated with school turnarounds can cut into teachers' personal lives. Much of the planning, meeting, and in-service training takes place after school, on Saturdays, and during the summer. When teachers have children of their own, it is hard to justify taking precious time away from family in order to help other parents' children. Whether or not teachers have families, they still need some "down time." Each teacher must arrive at his or her own conclusion about the demands required to turn around the school. In some cases, individuals will have to face up to the fact that they cannot make the commitment necessary to improve their school without sacrificing too much of their personal lives.

Threat to Job Security

It comes as no surprise that some teachers resist school turnaround initiatives because they fear losing their jobs. If a teacher has been teaching in a low-performing school for a while, she may feel vulnerable because she was associated with the preturnaround regime. Our studies of schools going through the turnaround process indicate that some teachers may be reassigned, nonrenewed, or fired. While the number of such actions in a given school is rarely more than a few, the fact remains that the school turnaround process is not without risk for teachers. It is important to acknowledge, however, that not undertaking a school turnaround in a perennially low-performing school also is risky. Under the provisions of the No Child Left Behind Act, such schools eventually are subject to reconstitution, in which case all teachers must reapply for their jobs, or even to being closed down.

SOME KEY ATTRIBUTES OF TEACHER CHANGE AGENTS

No one is in a better position to effect the changes needed to turn around a low-performing school than teachers. You and your colleagues occupy the front lines in the battle against ignorance. Without the active participation of most, if not all, of a school's faculty, the school stands no chance at all of improving student achievement. We have tried to convey a single, straightforward message throughout this book: teachers together can turn around a low-performing school. The task is certainly neither easy nor short-term, but it can be done. It *is* being done—in elementary, middle, and high schools across the country.

In this concluding section, we would like to highlight several of the attributes that are associated with successful teacher change agents.

An unwavering belief in the importance of public education is essential if teachers are to meet the challenges involved in turning around low-performing schools. As already has been noted, this process is rarely linear or smooth. There are plenty of detours and bumps in the road to raised achievement. Those unfortified by a commitment to the mission of public education may fall victim to discouragement and cynicism during times when school improvement efforts seem hopelessly stalled. Teachers faced with the frustrations of the change process should look into the eyes of their students and ask themselves, "Without a good education, what chance do they have?"

Teachers who thrive as change agents are able to resist the temptation to blame the victims. When children first attend school, they are rarely unmotivated, uncooperative, and resistant to learning. These reactions are learned over time. As a teacher, you can help to ensure that students continue to feel cared for and cared about. The temptation to regard students as problems when they fail to live up to our expectations must be seen for what it is—a reaction to feelings of disappointment and helplessness. No professional educator likes to feel helpless and unproductive. Such feelings, however, are predictable in low-performing schools. A constructive response to feeling helpless is to seek additional knowledge and skills in order to address students' difficulties.

This suggestion brings us to another attribute of teacher change agents. They are committed to the continuous improvement of instruction. Teaching is too complex ever to be fully mastered. Our knowledge of best practice is constantly evolving as we discover new research and confront new challenges. No teacher wants to see a physician who has failed to keep up with new developments in medicine. Teachers, too, must keep up with developments in their profession. It goes without saying that it is easier to do so when teachers cooperate and learn from and with each other.

No teacher can be an effective change agent unless he or she recognizes the necessity for teamwork. Teachers who have grown accustomed to working alone are likely to find teamwork to be a challenge. At first it can seem less efficient than doing things on one's own. But public education is a collective enterprise. As was noted at the beginning of this book, when a student walks across the stage at graduation and receives a diploma, it is because of the efforts of dozens of teachers. The more teachers cooperate, the more likely they are to meet the varying needs of all their students.

One other attribute should be mentioned before bringing this chapter to a close. Teacher change agents require confidence. Not the kind of confidence, though, that leads individuals to ignore what others have to say. The kind of confidence needed to turn around a low-performing school is the confidence of knowing that you will not give up. Such confidence derives from a combination of factors—a belief in the importance of your mission, a sincere commitment to those you serve, a willingness to continue searching for ways to be a better teacher, and faith in the collective efficacy of you and your colleagues.

> *Turnaround Tip::* For teacher change agents, there is no substitute for the kind of confidence that resists giving up, no matter how daunting the challenge.

FOLLOW-UP ACTIVITIES

1. If your school is considering a turnaround initiative, meet with your fellow teachers and identify all the possible sources of resistance to this initiative. For each source of resistance, try to provide one or more reasons for the resistance. Then brainstorm constructive ways to address the sources of resistance.
2. Reflect on your own experience with the change process, both on a personal level and professionally. Under what conditions are you most and least likely to change in a positive direction? When you have tried to change and not succeeded, what have been the difficulties that prevented you from changing? Can you think of ways to overcome these difficulties?
3. You can learn a great deal about yourself by keeping a journal during the first year of a school turnaround initiative. Set aside time every few days to write or tape record your reflections about the change process, how it is affecting you, and how you are affecting it. Try to identify sources of satisfaction, frustration, and challenge.

REFERENCES

Bridges, William. 2003. *Managing Transitions.* 2nd ed. Cambridge, MA: DaCapo Press.

Duke, Daniel L. 2004. *The Challenges of Educational Change.* Boston: Pearson.

Fullan, Michael. 2001. *Leading in a Culture of Change.* San Francisco: Jossey-Bass.

Fuller, Frances F. 1970. Personalized Education for Teachers: An Introduction for Teacher Educators. Austin: University of Texas, Research and Development Center for Teacher Education.

Hall, Gene E., and Shirley M. Hord. 2001. *Implementing Change*. Boston: Allyn and Bacon.

Kanter, Rosabeth Moss. 2004. *Confidence*. New York: Crown Business.

Knapp, Michael S., Michele C. Ferguson, Jerry D. Bamberg, and Paul T. Hill. 1998. Converging Reforms and the Working Lives of Front-Line Professionals in Schools. *Educational Policy* 12(4): 397–418.

Turnaround Resources

The purpose of this chapter is to provide additional resources to help you with your school's turnaround. Some resources are included in full. Others are described briefly so that you may determine if the entire resource would be useful.

The first section includes descriptions of school case study collections. The full case studies, available to you on the Internet, portray in rich detail the stories of schools that have met with newfound or against-the-odds academic success. The next section describes two multimedia presentations about school turnaround you can access online. The third section summarizes diagnostic instruments you can use in the turnaround process; many of the complete instruments are contained in the appendix. Fourth, we list books you may find both personally and professionally rewarding as you take part in change at your school. Next, we discuss some of the research resources pertaining to school turnarounds. In the last section, we list organizations involved with school turnaround and how to access their online resources.

CASE STUDIES OF TURNAROUND SCHOOLS

Elementary Schools

Charles A. Dana Center, University of Texas at Austin. 1999. *Hope for Urban Education: A Study of Nine High-Performing, High-Poverty, Urban*

Table 9.1.

Elementary Schools. Washington, DC: U.S. Department of Education, Planning and Evaluation Service.

Hope for Urban Education profiles nine public, high-poverty, urban elementary schools judged to be high performing because of reading and math test scores exceeding state and national averages. All nine had been low-performing prior to undergoing a change process that included (1) choosing and attaining an important but manageable goal, (2) redirecting energy toward serving children, (3) fostering an environment conducive to appropriate student behavior, (4) developing a shared sense of responsibility among staff members, (5) focusing on instructional leadership, (6) aligning instruction to standards and required assessments, (7) providing adequate materials and professional development, (8) coordinating shared planning time, (9) working toward improved relationships with parents, (10) adding instructional time, and (11) persisting in the face of challenge.

Baskin Elementary School

Baskin Elementary School in San Antonio, Texas, is one of the schools included in this collection. In 1998, the year of the case study, Baskin's student population was 6 percent African American, 1 percent Asian American, 75 percent Hispanic, and 18 percent White.

Challenges

Ninety-two percent of students were eligible for free or reduced-price lunch, 4.5 percent were English Language Learners, and Baskin had a 49 percent mobility rate. As the population shifted in the early 1990s, teachers continued with familiar practices that no longer yielded successful results for their students. Teachers simultaneously lowered expectations for some of their students. Test score data reflected racial achievement gaps.

Changes

The new state accountability system forced the Baskin staff to acknowledge the gap between White and non-White student test scores. The district focus sharpened on curriculum and instruction. In 1994, San Antonio's new superintendent reorganized the district into learning communities, replacing area superintendents with instructional stewards. The Baskin staff, also under new leadership in 1994, undertook a needs assessment. Together, the staff members designed a school reform framework that reflected the values of a professional learning community. The design consisted of "(1) distributed expertise and leadership; (2) curriculum organization, alignment, and assessment; (3) collective responsibility for student learning; (4) reflective dialogue; and (5) increased teacher efficacy" (46). While the principal took on the managerial responsibilities, including teacher evaluations, the administrative aid provided instructional support. Freed of the task of conducting teacher evaluations, she developed trusting relationships with teachers. The administrators addressed school climate with professional development and allocated time and space for collaboration. They created a workroom that teachers considered comparable to their favorite local bookstore. The schedule was altered to allow grade-level teachers to plan together and align curriculum. The school leaders sought parental connections by holding meetings at convenient times, providing childcare at evening meetings, creating videotapes of the school, and involving parents in the Instructional Leadership Team.

Outcomes

In 1994, only 44.4 percent of Baskin students passed the three sections of the Texas Assessment of Academic Skills. In 1998, 94.2 percent passed. In 2005, Baskin Elementary School was still maintaining its status as a high-poverty, high-performing school: 100 percent of Baskin third graders passed the Texas Assessment of Knowledge and Skills (TAKS) reading test, 97 percent of third graders passed the math test, 92 percent of fifth graders passed the reading test, and 95 percent of fifth graders passed the math test. All TAKS tests taken by third, fourth, fifth, and sixth graders in 2005 were passed by at least 90 percent of Baskin's students (Texas Education Agency website).

Hope for Urban Education is available at www.ed.gov/pubs/urbanhope/index.html.

Duke, Daniel L., et al. 2005. *Lift-off: Launching the School Turnaround Process in Ten Virginia Schools.* Charlottesville, VA: Partnership for Leaders in Education.

Lift-off tells the stories of the ten principals selected to participate in the inaugural year of the Virginia School Turnaround Specialist Program (VSTSP). The principals share what they encountered at their schools and their efforts to counter poor academic performance.

Woodville Elementary School

Woodville Elementary School in Richmond, Virginia, is one of the schools profiled in this collection of case studies. In 2005, the Woodville student population was 98.7 percent Black, 0.2 percent White, 0.2 percent Hispanic, and 0.8 percent other (SchoolMatters website, 2006).

Challenges

Woodville is located in an economically depressed neighborhood and serves many students residing in public housing projects. Over 75 percent of the student body was eligible for free or reduced-price lunch in 2005 and "weekend break-ins and lockdowns are not uncommon" at Woodville (56).

Changes

By combining resources from a strong community partnership and the VSTSP, the principal arranged for a staff retreat to examine Woodville's current status and plan for the future. Once the school year began, grade-level teams worked together during shared blocks of time. Choice of staff development topics was influenced by teacher input. Teachers adopted more active learning strategies and were trained in inclusion. Staff members combed through attendance, discipline, and test data—including benchmark test data—to determine differentiated instructional strategies, remediation plans, and other responses. Many of these before-school, during-school, and afterschool remediation and enrichment opportunities were made possible through community partnerships. The range of interventions and extent of resources allowed Woodville to provide almost every student with extra support. Woodville's powerful community partnerships have also made possible family and student field trips to cultural sites and special events in Richmond, children's summer camp attendance, and book clubs. Woodville faculty members also worked with the staff and residents of public housing communities where students live to encourage student attendance and parent involvement in the school. The PTA, dissolved under the previous principal due to counterproductive activities, was revived.

Outcomes

Virginia Standards of Learning test scores increased steadily between 2004 and 2006 for Woodville's third and fifth graders in both English and math. The percentage of third graders passing the English test rose from 63 percent to 98 percent. Seventy-three percent of third graders passed the math test in 2004; in 2006, 90 percent passed. The percentage of fifth graders passing the English test increased from 76 percent to 87 percent. Fifth graders passed the math test at a rate of 85 percent in 2004 and of 98 percent in 2006 (Virginia Department of Education website).

Lift-off is available online from the Darden/Curry Partnership for Leaders in Education Web site at www.dardencurry.org, specifically at www.darden .edu/uploadedFiles/Centers_of_Excellence/PLE/VSTPSFinal.pdf.

Middle Schools

Charles A. Dana Center, University of Texas at Austin. 2002. *Driven to Succeed: High-Performing, High-Poverty, Turnaround Middle Schools.* Vols. 1 and 2. Washington, DC: U.S. Department of Education, Planning and Evaluation Service.

Driven to Succeed profiles seven public, high-poverty middle schools designated as high performing because of reading and math test scores meeting or exceeding the state average and a strong growth rate between 1997 and 2000. The authors of the study identified four common themes that contributed to the success of the seven schools: high expectations for all students; collaboration among staff members, with the school district, and with outside organizations; galvanization of resources and thoughtful implementation of carefully chosen organizational structures; and individual student focus accompanied by targeted interventions.

Hambrick Middle School

Hambrick Middle School is located in Aldine, Texas, near Houston. In the 2000–2001 school year, 72 percent of Hambrick's 1,053 seventh and eighth graders were Hispanic, 21 percent were African American, and 6 percent were White.

Challenges

Principal Nancy Blackwell arrived at Hambrick to find low test scores, severe discipline issues, dropout problems, gang activity, isolated teachers, and a building in disrepair. Eighty percent of students were eligible for free or reduced-price lunch.

Changes

Blackwell's first move was to repair and clean the school building. She asked teachers what supplies they needed and was able to provide the needed supplies by reallocating Title I money. Students were no longer allowed to take two elective courses unless they had demonstrated sufficient mastery of core subjects. Money that previously supported the elective program was used to hire math teachers, allowing for smaller classes and more minutes spent in math. Bells and lockers were eliminated, and teachers monitored the hallways during passing time, cutting down on passing time chaos and the actual passing time needed. A consistently applied schoolwide discipline plan and the division of each grade level into three teams, each with its own hallway, contributed to a climate conducive to greater focus on instruction. Attention was paid to the progress of individual students in teachers' common planning time and during the careful assigning of each student's schedule. Before- and afterschool tutoring allowed students extra help. Teachers followed up with students who failed to attend those sessions. Students determined to be in need of mentoring were paired with a teacher. Teachers assessed student learning with benchmark testing and adjusted instruction according to the resultant data. The staff at Hambrick also used discipline data to make programmatic changes. All teachers were trained in gifted education, helping them to see the potential in all of their students.

Outcomes

By the 2000–2001 school year, Hambrick had all but eliminated the racial test-score gap with close to 100 percent of eighth graders passing the reading and math portions of the Texas Assessment of Academic Skills. Between the 1995–1996 school year and the 2000–2001 school year, the percentage of Hambrick students included in the gifted program jumped from 2.1 percent to 7 percent, 69 percent of whom were Hispanic, 17 percent African American, 14 percent White, and 64 percent eligible for free or reduced-price lunch. On the state test (TAKS) in 2005, 95 percent of seventh graders passed the reading test and 94 percent passed the math test. Ninety-five percent of eighth graders passed the reading test and 92 percent passed the math test (Texas Education Agency website).

Case collection available at www.utdanacenter.org.

High Schools

Werkema, R. D., and R. Case. 2005. Calculus as a Catalyst: The Transformation of an Inner-City High School in Boston. *Urban Education* 40(5): 497–520.

Jeremiah E. Burke High School

Jeremiah E. Burke High School is located in Boston, Massachusetts. In 2005, its student body was 81.4 percent African American, 13.2 percent Hispanic, 3.1 percent Asian/Pacific Islander, 1.8 percent White, and 0.5 percent American Indian/Alaska Native (SchoolMatters website, 2006).

Challenges

In 1995, Burke High School lost its accreditation. In 1998, Burke's tenth graders ranked last in the city on the Massachusetts Comprehensive Assessment System (MCAS). The building was in disrepair and students skipped classes. Students were served by only one guidance counselor and no librarian. Like many of its poor, inner-city peers, Burke High School's course offerings did not match the rigor of nearby suburban schools' offerings. Algebra I was the most advanced math class offered at Burke. Lack of access to higher-level courses limited Burke students' options for pursuing postsecondary education and jobs. According to the headmaster, over 75 percent of the study body was economically disadvantaged in 2005.

Changes

The headmaster determined a need for new behavioral norms and distributed responsibility throughout the building for creating new norms. The staff participated in extensive professional development to establish confidence in students' and teachers' capabilities. Advanced algebra and precalculus were added to the course catalog. AP Calculus was introduced in the fall of 1999.

Outcomes

From 1998 to 1999, Burke's MCAS scores increased at a greater rate than the district's scores. Based on the 2000 administration of MCAS, Burke ranked second among the twelve nonselective district high schools. In 2001, all of Burke's graduates were admitted to an institution of higher education.

CASE STUDIES OF HIGH-POVERTY/ HIGH-PERFORMING SCHOOLS

In addition to case studies of schools that have reversed poor performance, the literature abounds with stories of schools that are high poverty and high performing.

Charles A. Dana Center, University of Texas at Austin. 2001. *Opening Doors: Promising Lessons from Five Texas High Schools.*

The researchers selected for study five high-poverty Texas high schools with above-average performance on one or more academic achievement criteria, and notable improvement in state test scores. While the researchers discovered that each school implemented practices in accordance with its own unique context, the schools all set clear goals and high expectations, used data to inform instructional decisions, focused on instruction and individual student progress, supported teachers, broadened and deepened collaboration, and fostered an environment of care and respect for students. They conclude their study with a list of recommendations for both school and district leaders.

Case collection available at www.utdanacenter.org/. www.utdanacenter.org/downloads/products/openingdoors/hscrosscase .pdf

Education Trust. November 2005. The Power to Change: High Schools that Help All Students Achieve.

This Education Trust study profiles two high-performing schools and one fast-improving school, all with student bodies of primarily minority and low-income students. The authors found that the staffs of all three high schools used data to inform decision making, focused their attentions on instruction, connected students with adults in the school, and shared the belief that all students can learn.

Case collection available at www.edtrust.org.

Manset, G., et al. 2000. *Wisconsin's High-Performing/High-Poverty Schools.* Indiana Education Policy Center

Researchers conducted case studies of six high-performing, high-poverty (HP/HP) schools in Wisconsin in order to identify the features driving their success. They identified seventeen such features in the five categories of implementation of a philosophy, staff development, parent and community involvement, instruction, and classroom organization. Students identified as economically disadvantaged in the HP/HP schools achieved higher test scores than their economically disadvantaged peers in other Wisconsin schools. Students at five of the six schools intended to attend college at rates similar to their peers. In addition to studying these six schools, the researchers surveyed teachers at both HP/HP schools and at schools beginning comprehensive school reform, determining similarities and differences between the two groups of teachers.

McGee, G. W. 2004. Closing the Achievement Gap: Lessons from Illinois' Golden Spike High-Poverty High-Performing Schools. *Journal of Education for Students Placed at Risk* 9(2): 97–125.

Author Glenn McGee locates high-poverty schools that are also high achieving, and describes the factors that contribute to their success. Over 90 percent of these "Golden Spike" schools shared the following features: strong leadership advocating for a culture of success, an early literacy focus, teachers who believe all children can learn, more time learning academic subjects, and parent involvement. McGee offers several policy recommendations: prioritize educational achievement for children of low-income families, fund early reading interventions, fund parent-involvement programming, increase time in school, provide team training for educators involved with high-poverty schools, and expand school services to include parent education and health services.

Case collection available at http://eric.ed.gov/.

Kannapel, P. J., and S. K. Clements. 2005. *Inside the Black Box of High-Performing High-Poverty Schools.* Lexington, KY: Prichard Committee for Academic Excellence.

Kannapel and Clements examined eight high-performing elementary schools with 50 percent or more students eligible for free or reduced-price lunch. At all eight schools, they found high expectations, respectful relationships among staff and students, focus on instruction, instructional adjustment based upon regular assessment of learning, collaborative decision making, strong faculty work ethic, and careful attention to teacher hiring and assignment. Based on their observations, the authors suggest further study to inform policy in the following areas: routine assessment of individual student learning; cultivating quality personnel; the role of poverty; and curriculum, instruction, and assessment alignment.

Case collection available at www.prichardcommittee.org/Ford%20Study/ FordReportJE.pdf.

SCHOOL TURNAROUND: MULTIMEDIA

Public Broadcasting System (PBS)—The NewsHour with Jim Lehrer

Thomas Boushall Middle School in Richmond, Virginia, is profiled in a four-part series on a school turnaround. Education journalist John Merrow reports on the challenges facing the school's teachers and principal Parker Land, a participant in the VSTSP.

Story and video available online at www.pbs.org/merrow/tv/newshour/ turnaround4.html.

PBS—"Turnaround Specialist Roundtable"

Education journalist John Merrow discusses the school turnaround process with three principals in the Virginia School Turnaround Specialist Program.

Listen to the podcast online at www.merrow.org/podcast/56.mp3. Download the transcript from www.pbs.org/merrow/podcast/index.html.

DIAGNOSTIC INSTRUMENTS[1]

Need for Change Assessment

A prerequisite for turning around a school is recognizing a need for change. The PnC survey was designed to assess teachers' perceived need for change in how their school promotes academic achievement.

For example, what specific aspects of the reading program are weak and require improvement? Is data used adequately to inform instructional decisions? Teachers respond to twenty-five questions with a rating of one through four. The survey results can be aggregated to paint a picture of how the faculty perceives the academic program of the school.

Conditions Associated with Low Performance in Schools

Through our research, we have found that a school in need of turnaround has its own unique set of challenging conditions. Identify your school's performance profile guided by this checklist of conditions found in low-performing schools in order to determine where to focus your energies.

Student Assessment of Learning Environment (SALE)

Student voices are often absent from school improvement efforts. The SALE survey was designed to determine how students feel about their school. Students in grades three through twelve respond to twenty questions with a rating of one through three. With the compiled results of SALE, school turnaround efforts can take student perspectives into account.

First Steps

To undertake informed change, it is important to have a detailed understanding of a school's current status. The First Steps questionnaire guides faculty members through a detailed analysis of the state of reading and math instruction, personnel issues, discipline, and organizational structure.

What Works

What Works and What Doesn't Work with School Turnarounds provides descriptions of successful and unsuccessful efforts to establish a mission, collect and analyze data, collaborate, schedule, provide staff development, and implement interventions. Compare the practices at your school with what has been found to work and not to work in various school turnaround initiatives.

School Improvement Program Needs Assessment Questionnaire (1987)

Elementary School Authors: Dodson, A. G., et al.
Middle School Author: Dodson, A. G.
Secondary School Authors: Dodson, A. G., Lezotte, L., and Shoemaker, J.
This questionnaire examines school effectiveness from the perspectives of students, teachers, staff, and parents. It rates perceived effectiveness in a variety of areas, including administration, climate, mission, community relations, parental involvement, student expectations, academic skills, monitoring of academic progress, and resource allocation. Elementary, middle, and high school versions of the questionnaire are available.

Available from Test Collection, Educational Testing Service, Princeton, NJ 08541, www.ets.org
ETS Call Numbers: TC015982 (Elementary School); TC015983 (Middle School); TC015984 (High School)

Teachers' Beliefs about Administrators Scale (1988)

Authors: Feldman, D. and Gerstein, L. H.
This instrument measures teachers' beliefs about administrators at their schools. The results of this test can be used to improve teacher-administrator relationships.

This diagnostic tool is not readily accessible via Internet, but may be accessed at university or public library databases.

School Assessment Survey (1985)

Author: Wilson, B. L.
This instrument assesses elementary and secondary school organizational conditions that support school improvement and overall school effectiveness. This survey examines nine school climate areas, including administrative leadership, classroom instruction, discipline, and staff conflict.

Available from Research for Better Schools, 444 North Third Street, Philadelphia, PA 19123, www.rbs.org
ETS Call Number: TC015265

Spectrum: An Organizational Development Tool (1985)

Authors: Braskamp, L. A. and Maehr, M. L.
This instrument examines teachers' beliefs about their school culture, professional commitments, and job satisfaction. This tool may be used to understand what motivates individual faculty members in your school.

This diagnostic tool is not readily accessible via Internet, but may be accessed at university or public library databases.

Assessment of School Needs for Low-Achieving Students (1988)

Authors: Beyer, F. S. and Houston, R. L.
This instrument identifies faculty knowledge and skill deficits in working with low-achieving students. The assessment is completed by both teachers and administrators, and the results can be used to help determine school improvement efforts to assist low-achieving students.

This diagnostic tool is not readily accessible via Internet, but may be accessed at university or public library databases.

PERSONAL INSPIRATION

Johnson, S. 1998. *Who Moved My Cheese?: An Amazing Way to Deal with Change in Your Work and in Your Life*. New York: G. P. Putnam's Sons.

"Read the book 'Who Moved My Cheese?' by Spencer Johnson," recommended Dave Oland, social studies teacher at Wyandotte High School, a school undergoing the turnaround process. "It should be required reading for all staff members who are going through the reform process" (National Education Association 2002, 8).

Johnson's tale of mice, men, and cheese tackles the strong beliefs about ourselves and the world we cling to in the face of change, often to our detriment. In this quick read, Johnson conveys the powerful message that if we meet change with a clear eye, change can give us opportunities to thrive in new ways.

Quinn, R. E. 1996. *Deep Change: Discovering the Leader Within.* 1st ed. San Francisco, CA: Jossey-Bass.

Quinn argues that lasting, transformational change requires taking risk and relinquishing control, unlike the relatively mundane requirements of incremental change. And, deep change in an organization requires deep personal change in its members.

Collins, J. 2001. *Good to Great.* New York: HarperCollins.

Jim Collins maintains that "good is the enemy of great" (1). To determine how to make the jump from good to great, Collins and his team researched both good companies and great companies that were once good companies. In *Good to Great*, they identify what it is that great companies do to move from being good to being great, hoping to impart to their readers the belief that all have the potential to make the change.

Covey, S. R. 2000. *Living the Seven Habits: The Courage to Change.* New York: Fireside.

Stephen Covey shares the stories of people who have used the seven habits identified in his earlier work, *The Seven Habits of Highly Effective People*, to make important change in their lives. This book includes a section on teachers and schools.

Lundin, S. C., H. Paul, and J. Christensen. 2000. *Fish! A Remarkable Way to Boost Morale and Improve Results.* New York: Hyperion.

Borrowing lessons from the famous Pike Place Fish Market in Seattle, the authors tell the fictional tale of Mary Jane Ramirez and her efforts to transform a poorly performing office. They showcase changes in perspective that translate into happiness and excitement in the workplace.

SCHOOL TURNAROUND RESEARCH

Copland, M. A., and E. Boatright. December 2006. *Leadership for Transforming High Schools.* Retrieved February 26, 2007, from the University of Washington, Center for the Study of Teaching and Policy website: http://depts.washington.edu/ctpmail/PDFs/HighSchool-Dec13.pdf.

The authors of this study argue that the current model of the American high school still reflects the century-old comprehensive school designed to sort and select students. They contend that the present-day high school should instead focus on providing each student with a strong education. To counteract a tendency to maintain the structural and cultural status quo, the authors recommend that school leaders focus on learning, use data in decision making, align resources with learning goals, reconfigure leadership positions to emphasize instructional leadership, involve the community, and distribute leadership across the school staff. They identify three types of change that surface in high school reform efforts: change in structural design, change in instructional practice, and the creation of a greater array of choices.

Duke, D. L. n.d. *Keys to Sustaining Successful School Turnarounds.* Retrieved March 8, 2007, from the University of Virginia, Darden/Curry Partnership for Leaders in Education website: www.darden.edu/uploaded Files/Centers_of_Excellence/PLE/KeysToSuccess.pdf.

In this paper, the author explores the lasting changes evident in fifteen elementary schools that have sustained success for at least two years after their initial turnaround. After an in-depth discussion of specific changes in all aspects of school function, the author concludes that systemic change, customized change, and a base of essential changes are required for sustained success.

EdSource. June 2006. *Similar Students, Different Results: Why Do Some Schools Do Better?* Retrieved February 26, 2007, from www.edsource.org/pdf/simstusumm06.pdf.

By selecting California schools that fell between the twenty-fifth and thirty-fifth percentiles of the School Characteristics Index, the researchers identified a pool of schools with similar student populations. The schools in that pool were divided into low-, medium-, and high-performing based upon the Academic Performance Index (API). Principals and teachers at the schools completed surveys detailing school practices. Comparing these survey responses, the researchers discovered a correlation between higher API scores and an emphasis on student achievement, a standards-based curriculum, data-informed instruction, and sufficient instructional resources. The study authors conclude that school practices can impact student achievement.

Harris, D. N. 2006. *Ending the Blame Game on Educational Inequity: A Study of "High-Flying" Schools and NCLB.* Retrieved February 23, 2007 from Arizona State University, Education Policy Research Unit website: http://epsl.asu.edu/epru/.

Educational economist Douglas Harris reviews studies undertaken by the Educational Trust and the Heritage Foundation that point to large numbers of high-poverty, high-performing schools. Harris critiques their methods and definitions of high performing, questioning their conclusions that either schools or the children themselves are to blame. The report concludes with policy recommendations that acknowledge community and family factor influences on academic achievement.

Study available online at http://epsl.asu.edu/epru/documents/EPSL-0603-120-EPRU.pdf.

National Education Association. September 2002. *Making Low-Performing Schools a Priority: An Association Research Guide.* Retrieved February 26, 2007, from http://www.nea.org/priorityschools/images/PSI2002Resource Guide-low.pdf.

This NEA research guide offers recommendations and tools for turning around low-performing schools and maintaining their newfound success. The guide highlights schools that have successfully implemented some of the suggestions shared in the guide. Included is a list of monetary and informational resources to aid in school improvement efforts.

Public Impact. 2005. *School Restructuring Options under No Child Left Behind: What Works When? Turnarounds with New Leaders and Staff.* Retrieved February 26, 2007, from www.centerforcsri.org/pubs/restructuring/KnowledgeIssues4Turnaround.pdf.

A literature review revealed similarities between the elements of non-education turnaround and school turnaround, though practical limitations and the politics of school environments create additional challenges. The authors identify four categories of factors that impact turnaround efforts. Governance factors include accountability, support, aligned systems, and permission to take action. The roles and involvement of the community define environmental factors. Leadership factors include the defined role of the principal and characteristics of successful turnaround leaders. Organizational factors involve staff, culture, and school design.

United Kingdom National Audit Office. January 11, 2006. *Improving Poorly Performing Schools in England.* Retrieved February 26, 2007, from http://www.nao.org.uk/publications/nao_reports/05-06/0506679.pdf.

In this report, England's National Audit Office examines in detail the process of identifying and providing support for poorly performing schools, efforts to turn around these schools, and the requirements of sustaining high performance. Based on their research, the authors identify practical steps that the education department, local governing authorities, and schools can take to improve schools.

ORGANIZATIONS

The American Association of School Administrators (AASA), a professional organization of educational leaders, promotes high quality public education for every student. www.aasa.org

The American Federation of Teachers (AFT), a union of education workers, "advocates sound, commonsense public education policies, including high academic and conduct standards for students and greater professionalism for teachers and school staff." www.aft.org

The Association for Supervision and Curriculum Development (ASCD) is "a community of educators, advocating sound policies and sharing best practices to achieve the success of each learner." www.ascd.org

The Council of Chief State School Officers (CCSSO) is a nonprofit organization of public education officials that "provides leadership, advocacy, and technical assistance on major educational issues." www.ccsso.org

The Darden/Curry Partnership for Leaders in Education aims to provide "innovative solutions to education leaders by merging best practices from business and education." www.dardencurry.org

The Education Trust works toward high academic achievement for all students. www.edtrust.org

The National Association of Elementary School Principals (NAESP) engages in "advocacy and support for elementary and middle level principals and other education leaders in their commitment to all children." www.naesp.org

The National Association of Secondary School Principals (NASSP) promotes "excellence in middle and high school leadership." www.principals.org

The National Education Association (NEA), an advocacy organization for public school employees, aims for "great public schools for every child." www.nea.org

The National School Boards Association (NSBA) promotes "excellence and equity in public education through school board leadership." www.nsba.org

Public Impact, an education policy and management consulting firm, aims to "improve student learning in K–12 education." www.publicimpact.com

The Wallace Foundation disseminates information about and financially supports education leadership. www.wallacefoundation.org

WestEd, a nonprofit research, development, and service agency, aims for all to experience success in learning. www.wested.org

ENDNOTE

1. See Appendix A for the first five diagnostic instruments included in this section.

REFERENCES

National Education Association. 2002. *Making Low-Performing Schools a Priority: An Association Research Guide*. September. Retrieved February 26, 2007, from www.nea.org/priorityschools/images/PSI2002ResourceGuide-low.pdf.

SchoolMatters: A Service of Standard & Poor's Website. 2006. *Burke High School*. Retrieved March 18, 2007, from www.schoolmatters.com.

SchoolMatters: A Service of Standard & Poor's Website. 2006. *Woodville Elementary*. Retrieved February 18, 2007, from www.schoolmatters.com.

Texas Education Agency Website. *Student Assessment Division: TAKS Aggregate Data System*. Retrieved March 23, 2007, from www.tea.state.tx.us/student .assessment/reporting/taksagg/index.html.

Virginia Department of Education Website. *Woodville Elementary*. Retrieved February 12, 2007, from https://p1pe.doe.virginia.gov/reportcard/report.do? division=All&schoolName=211.

Appendix A

Need for Change Assessment*

Below are listed various changes that have been associated with efforts to improve student achievement. Read both ends of the scale for each item, then consider your school and circle the number on the four-point scale that best represents your feelings.

1) Struggling readers at this school need additional instructional time on reading.   1 2 3 4   They have enough instructional time for reading now.

2) Teachers at this school need to spend more time reviewing student performance data.   1 2 3 4   Teachers spend enough time reviewing data now.

3) Our reading program is not well suited to the needs of our students.   1 2 3 4   Our reading program is very well suited to students' needs.

4) We need a new approach to discipline.   1 2 3 4   Our current approach to discipline is effective.

5) Our math program is not well suited to the needs of our students.   1 2 3 4   Our math program is well suited to students' needs.

6) We should do more to encourage better student attendance.   1 2 3 4   Our efforts to encourage student attendance are sufficient.

7) We need better interventions to assist low achievers.   1 2 3 4   Our approaches to assisting low achievers are sufficient.

8) We need more specialists to assist teachers.   1 2 3 4   There are an adequate number of specialists.

*This survey instrument was constructed with the generous financial support of the Microsoft Corporation.

9) Teachers need to engage in more collaboration/teamwork.	1 2 3 4	Teachers collaborate sufficiently.
10) This school needs more parent involvement.	1 2 3 4	Parents' level of involvement is sufficient.
11) Teachers should do more to differentiate instruction for students of different ability levels.	1 2 3 4	Teachers already differentiate instruction sufficiently.
12) Special education students should be included more in regular classrooms.	1 2 3 4	Special education students are included in regular classrooms to a sufficient extent.
13) More teachers at this school should be involved in teaching reading.	1 2 3 4	Only language arts/reading teachers should teach reading.
14) This school needs more partnerships with community groups.	1 2 3 4	This school has sufficient community partnerships.
15) Students need more instruction in how to take standardized tests.	1 2 3 4	Current instruction in how to take standardized tests is sufficient.
16) Teachers should spend more time aligning instruction with the content of state tests and state curriculum standards.	1 2 3 4	Teachers spend sufficient time on alignment.
17) Students need to take more interim (benchmark) tests so teachers can monitor progress more closely.	1 2 3 4	Students take a sufficient number of benchmark tests.
18) Teachers need to learn how to use classroom assessment to support student learning.	1 2 3 4	Teachers know how to use classroom assessment to support learning.
19) Struggling students should receive more targeted (individualized) assistance prior to taking standardized tests.	1 2 3 4	Students currently receive an appropriate amount of targeted assistance.
20) Instructional planning needs to be more data driven.	1 2 3 4	Instructional planning is sufficiently data driven.
21) Some teachers need to be reassigned in order to increase instructional effectiveness.	1 2 3 4	Current teacher assignments provide maximum effectiveness.
22) The school schedule should be changed to permit more effective instruction and assistance for struggling students.	1 2 3 4	The current school schedule is sufficient.

23) Changes are needed in how students are grouped for instruction.   1 2 3 4   Current student grouping is sufficient.

24) Professional development should be more closely tied to the needs of students at this school.   1 2 3 4   Professional development is sufficient as is.

25) The district should provide more support for what we do at this school.   1 2 3 4   The district provides adequate support for what we do.

Are there changes that you feel must be made in order to raise student achievement in this school?
If so, please list them below.

Date _____

School _____

Appendix B

Conditions Associated with
Low Performance in Schools

These conditions were present in my school to the following degree:	Not Present	Somewhat Present	Fully Present
Student Achievement and Behavior:			
Low Reading Achievement			
Low Math Achievement			
Attendance Problems			
Discipline Problems			
School Programs and Organization:			
Lack of Focus			
Unaligned Curriculum			
Data Deprivation			
Lack of Teamwork			
Inadequate Infrastructure			
Ineffective Scheduling			
Dysfunctional Culture			
Ineffective Interventions			
Lack of Inclusion			
Inadequate Facilities			
Inadequate Materials			
Ineffective Staff Development			
Ineffective Instruction			
Staffing:			
Personnel Problems			
Lack of Specialists			

(continued)

These conditions were present in my school to the following degree:	Not Present	Somewhat Present	Fully Present
School System:			
Central Office Instability			
Technical Difficulties			
Lack of District Support			
School-District Coordination Issues			
Parents and Community			
Low Parent Involvement			
Community Negative Perceptions			

Name _____   Date _____

School _____

Partnership for
Leaders in Education

UNIVERSITY of VIRGINIA

Appendix C

Student Assessment of Learning Environment (SALE) Grades 3–5

Information about Me

Circle One:	Circle One:	Circle One:
I am a boy.	I am African American.	I am in 3rd grade.
I am a girl.	I am Asian or Pacific.	I am in 4th grade.
	I am Hispanic.	I am in 5th grade.
	I am White.	

Directions: Color in the face for each sentence.

What do you think?	Yes	I'm not sure	No
My teachers always help me when I need it.	☺	😐	☹
I like coming to school.	☺	😐	☹
My teachers care about how I'm doing in school.	☺	😐	☹
My teachers expect me to work hard and do my best.	☺	😐	☹
The work I do in school is interesting.	☺	😐	☹

What do you think?	*Yes*	*I'm not sure*	*No*
I learn new things in my classes.	☺	😐	☹
I feel safe in this school.	☺	😐	☹
My teachers show respect to all students.	☺	😐	☹
My teachers use many ways to teach.	☺	😐	☹
My teachers listen to student ideas.	☺	😐	☹

What do you think?	*Yes*	*I'm not sure*	*No*
My teachers give us extra practice to help us learn.	☺	😐	☹
My teachers make sure we learn new things.	☺	😐	☹
My teachers get everyone to like learning.	☺	😐	☹
My teachers go over what we learned earlier.	☺	😐	☹
My teachers give us extra help during lunch and after school if we need it.	☺	😐	☹

What do you think?	*Yes*	*I'm not sure*	*No*
Awards are given for coming to school and doing good work.	☺	😐	☹
Teachers talk to my parents about how I'm doing in school.	☺	😐	☹
My teachers make sure students understand what we are learning.	☺	😐	☹
Students in my classes care about learning.	☺	😐	☹
Students behave themselves in my classes most of the time.	☺	😐	☹

Partnership for
Leaders in Education

UNIVERSITY *of* VIRGINIA

Appendix D

Student Assessment of Learning Environment (SALE) Grades 6–12

Student Information:

Grade

6th ⬭	10th ⬭	African American ⬭	Male ⬭	
7th ⬭	11th ⬭	Asian/Pacific ⬭	Female ⬭	
8th ⬭	12th ⬭	Hispanic ⬭		
9th ⬭		White ⬭		

Choose **"I agree"** or **"I'm not sure"** or **"I don't agree"** for each statement. Color in the ⬭ under your choice.

Give your opinion about the following:	I agree	I'm not sure	I don't agree
My teachers always help me when I need it.	⬭	⬭	⬭
I look forward to coming to school.	⬭	⬭	⬭
My teachers care about how I'm doing in school.	⬭	⬭	⬭
My teachers expect me to work hard and do my best.	⬭	⬭	⬭
The work I do in school is interesting.	⬭	⬭	⬭
I learn new things in my classes.	⬭	⬭	⬭
I feel safe in this school.	⬭	⬭	⬭
My teachers show respect to all students.	⬭	⬭	⬭

(continued)

Give your opinion about the following:	I agree	I'm not sure	I don't agree
My teachers use many ways to teach.	⬭	⬭	⬭
My teachers listen to student ideas.	⬭	⬭	⬭
My teachers give us extra practice to help us learn.	⬭	⬭	⬭
My teachers make sure we learn new material.	⬭	⬭	⬭
My teachers get everyone involved in learning.	⬭	⬭	⬭
My teachers review what we learned earlier in the year.	⬭	⬭	⬭
My teachers give us help at lunch and after school if we need it.	⬭	⬭	⬭
Students get awards for coming to school and doing good work.	⬭	⬭	⬭
Teachers talk to my parents about how I'm doing in school.	⬭	⬭	⬭
My teachers make sure students understand what we are learning.	⬭	⬭	⬭
Students in my classes care about learning.	⬭	⬭	⬭
Students behave themselves in my classes most of the time.	⬭	⬭	⬭

Appendix E

First Steps: A Diagnostic Tool for School Turnaround Specialists[1]

Developed by the
RESEARCH TEAM
of the
Darden/Curry Partnership for Leaders in Education
2005

1. Reading

   1.1. Over the past five years, has reading achievement, as measured by standardized tests, declined, improved, or fluctuated?

   1.2. Over the past five years, has the percentage of students identified as low readers declined, increased, or fluctuated?

   1.3. Does your school use one or more reading series? If so, which reading series is/are in use? How long has each series been in use?

   1.4. What special programs and/or sources of assistance outside of the regular classroom are available to low readers?

   How long has each one been in existence at this school?

   During the last school year, how many students participated in each program or received each type of assistance?

   What percentage of students in each program showed evidence of improved reading by the end of the last school year?

[1]These materials were developed with the generous financial support of the Microsoft Corporation.

What percentage of the students receiving each type of assistance showed evidence of improved reading by the end of the last school year?

1.5. Does it appear, based on the data, that certain reading interventions (programs, sources of assistance) are not particularly effective? Which ones?

1.6. Were there students last school year who needed help with reading but who did not receive any assistance outside of the regular classroom? If so, approximately how many?

1.7. When student performance on standardized tests of reading is analyzed, do particular reading skills tend to be deficient (i.e., comprehension, vocabulary, word attack skills, etc.)? If so, which ones?

Are the areas of reading deficiency identified above being addressed in a systematic way (1) by classroom teachers and/or (2) in special programs? Provide an indication of how each deficiency is being addressed.

2. Mathematics

2.1. Over the past five years, has math achievement, as measured by standardized tests, declined, improved, or fluctuated?

2.2. Over the past five years, has the percentage of students identified as low math ability students declined, increased, or fluctuated?

2.3. Does your school use one or more math textbook series? If so, which series is/are in use? How long has each series been in use?

2.4. What special programs and/or sources of assistance outside of the regular classroom are available to students who are performing poorly in math?

How long has each one been in existence at this school?

During the last school year, how many students participated in each program or received each type of assistance?

What percentage of students in each program showed evidence of improved math achievement by the end of the last school year?

What percentage of the students receiving each type of assistance showed evidence of improved math achievement by the end of the last school year?

2.5. Does it appear, based on the data, that certain math interventions (programs, sources of assistance) are not particularly effective? Which ones?

2.6. Were there students last school year who needed help with math but who did not receive any assistance outside of the regular classroom? If so, approximately how many?

2.7. When student performance on standardized tests of mathematics is analyzed, do particular math skills tend to be deficient? If so, which ones?

Are the areas of math deficiency identified above being addressed in a systematic way (1) by classroom teachers and/or (2) in special programs? Provide an indication of how each deficiency is being addressed.

3. Personnel

3.1. Current Staff

What is the size of your faculty?

_____ Number of full-time teachers

_____ Number of part-time teachers

_____ Number of full-time administrators

_____ Number of support staff members

How many teachers are probationary (nontenured)? _____

How many teachers lack appropriate teaching credentials? _____

How many teachers were hired this year? _____

How many teachers currently are on a plan of assistance? _____

3.2. Staffing Needs

Are additional staff needed at this school? If so, specify the positions for which additional staff are needed.

4. Discipline and Attendance

4.1. Organization

Is a schoolwide discipline plan currently in place? If so, how long has it been in place? What are its components?

Is a schoolwide attendance plan currently in place? If so, how long has it been in place? What are its components?

4.2. Student Misbehavior

How many referrals have been given to misbehaving students in each of the past two years?

How many students had multiple referrals in each of the past two years?

In the past two years combined, what are the top two reasons for which students have received referrals?

How many students have received suspensions in each of the past two years?

How many students have been expelled in each of the past two years? For what were they expelled?

In the past two years, have a disproportionate number of referrals come from a small number of teachers?

In the past two years, have referrals been properly reported by teachers and administrators?

4.3. Consequences

Are any of the consequences for misbehavior or poor attendance seen as ineffective in correcting problems?

5. Teacher Teams

5.1. Leadership Team

Is there a designated leadership team?   YES   NO

Who is on the leadership team? (Indicate the positions they hold, not their names.)

How were members of the leadership team selected?

Appointed   Elected   Combination

How often does the leadership team meet?

_____ Once a week

_____ More than once a week

_____ Once a month

_____ Less than once a month

What are the primary responsibilities of the leadership team?

5.2. Grade-level Teams

Are teachers organized into grade-level teams?   YES   NO

How often do grade-level teams meet?

What are the primary responsibilities of grade-level teams?

5.3. Subject-Matter/Curriculum Teams

Are teachers organized into subject-matter or curriculum teams?

_____ Every teacher is on at least one subject-matter team

_____ Some teachers are on at least one subject-matter team

_____ No subject-matter teams exist

What are the primary responsibilities of subject-matter teams?

5.4. Intervention and Other Special Teams

Do other teams exist? If so, specify the name of each team, its membership, and its primary responsibilities:

6. Monitoring Student Learning in Preparation for State Testing

6.1. Were benchmark tests aligned with state testing administered in the past year? If so, to which groups of students and with what frequency?

6.2. Do teachers of the same grade or subject matter meet to determine the items on which students will be tested on teacher-made tests? Do the teachers meet to analyze the results?

7. Professional and Staff Development

7.1. What types of professional and staff development did teachers participate in during the past year?

- District staff development
- In-school professional and/or staff development
- In-classroom professional and/or staff development

7.2. What topics were covered in professional and staff development?

7.3. For which professional and staff development opportunities was there follow-up? What form did it take?

7.4. Are there any discernible outcomes from last year's professional development opportunities? What were they?

7.5. Did teachers find these professional development opportunities worthwhile? In what ways?

7.6. Based on the assessment of the previous year's professional and staff development, what are the current professional development needs?

8. Alignment

8.1. Do all teachers of the same subject follow the same curriculum?

8.2. Are the curricula in core areas aligned with state tests?

8.3. Are benchmark tests aligned with the curriculum and the end-of-year standardized tests?

8.4. Are instructional strategies aligned with curricular goals?

8.5. Are academic interventions aligned with the schoolwide academic goals?

8.6. Are the curriculum and instructional strategies of the interventions aligned with those of the school?

8.7. Are staffing patterns aligned with schoolwide academic goals?

8.8. Is the school schedule aligned with schoolwide academic goals?

8.9. Is professional development aligned with schoolwide academic goals?

8.10. Is the work of teacher teams focused on the schoolwide academic goals?

8.11. Are standardized test results analyzed for error patterns that may reflect lack of curricular alignment?

Appendix F

What Works and What Doesn't Work with School Turnarounds?[1]

Developed by the
RESEARCH TEAM
of the
Darden-Curry Partnership for Leaders in Education[2]

	What Works	**What Doesn't Work**
MISSION	1. Academically focused targets 2. Specific, measurable focus 3. Challenging, but achievable targets 4. Relatively few targets	1. Vague or highly generalized 2. Conflicting targets 3. Impossible or unrealistic targets 4. Too many targets
COLLECTION AND ANALYSIS OF DATA	1. Regular administration of benchmark assessments to monitor progress in achieving academic targets 2. Frequent review and strategic planning in response to assessment results	1. Annual assessment of student learning 2. Faculty review of test results from previous year

(continued)

[1]This research report was produced through the generous financial support of the Microsoft Corporation.

[2]Members of the Research Team include Daniel Duke, Pamela Tucker, Michael Salmonowicz, Melissa Levy, and Carolyn Pinkerton.

	What Works	**What Doesn't Work**
COLLABORATION	1. Staff discusses student achievement data on a regular basis 2. Staff determines how to assist struggling students 3. Staff monitors curriculum content to ensure vertical and horizontal alignment	1. Staff collectively denies responsibility for low academic achievement 2. Staff collectively resists efforts to improve instruction 3. Staff maintains individual autonomy and refuses to collaborate
SCHEDULING	Daily schedules that provide additional learning time in core subjects for struggling students	Longer blocks of time when teachers continue to teach the way they previously taught
STAFF DEVELOPMENT	1. Training focused on specific academic improvement targets 2. Post-training coaching and monitoring by highly trained experts	1. Brief in-service programs on a broad variety of general topics 2. "One-shot" workshops with no coaching or other follow-up activities
INTERVENTIONS	1. Interventions that require specialist to work in tandem with regular classroom teachers 2. Interventions where trained volunteers are closely supervised by qualified teachers 3. Interventions that target each student's deficiencies 4. Tutoring supports classroom instruction	1. Interventions that rely heavily on students being pulled out of regular classes in core subjects 2. Interventions that depend on untrained volunteers and unqualified teachers 3. Interventions that require students to be retaught material they already have mastered 4. Tutoring that is not aligned to current curriculum content

About the Authors

Daniel L. Duke has been a high school social studies teacher, a secondary school administrator, a program development specialist for a Teacher Corps project, a consultant to over 150 school systems and government agencies, and a prolific author. For the past 32 years he has served as a professor of educational leadership at Lewis and Clark College, Stanford University, and the University of Virginia. The author of 27 books and over 200 articles, book chapters, and research reports, Duke's recent publications include *The Challenges of Educational Change*, *Education Empire: The Evolution of an Excellent Suburban School System*, and *The Little School System That Could: Transforming a City School District*. Duke has served as President of the University Council for Educational Administration and helped to create the Thomas Jefferson Center for Educational Design and the Partnership for Leaders in Education (a center dedicated to turning around low-performing schools and school systems). Duke's academic interests include school improvement, educational change, and leader development.

Pamela D. Tucker is Associate Professor and Vice Chair of the Educational Leadership, Foundations, and Policy Department in the Curry School of Education at the University of Virginia. This is her tenth year in higher education following 13 years as a K-12 teacher and school administrator. As a practitioner, Dr. Tucker worked with a variety of student populations and served as a special education teacher and administrator, coordinator for a state-level homeless education program, and an advocate for elementary alternative education programs. She is active in professional organizations at the state and national level that promote educational leadership for schools. Her research on teacher effectiveness, school leadership and school improvement has been published in journals such as *Educational Administration Quarterly, Journal of Personnel Evaluation in Education, Leadership and Policy in Schools, Educational Leadership,* and *The School Administrator.* Books co-authored with others include: *Linking Teacher Evaluation and Student Achievement* (2005), *Handbook for the Qualities of Effective Teachers* (2004), and *Educational Leadership in an Age of Accountability* (2003).

Michael J. Salmonowicz taught high school English in Chicago, Illinois as a Teach For America corps member, and currently is a doctoral candidate in educational administration and supervision at the University of Virginia's Curry School of Education. As a research assistant and consultant with UVa's Partnership for Leaders in Education, Salmonowicz has researched the work of "turnaround principals" in four states and conducted instructional reviews of under-performing districts in two others. He is author or co-author of a number of articles, case studies, and research reports dealing with the change process in low-performing schools, school district policies, and methods of raising and sustaining student achievement. Salmonowicz earned a bachelor's degree in English from the University of Michigan, and a master's degree in teaching from National-Louis University.

Melissa K. Levy has worked and volunteered with students in grades K-16 as a music teacher, tutor, and adviser, and is currently a doctoral student in social foundations of education at the University of Virginia's Curry School of Education. Levy's research is focused on the relationship between intervention programs and the "at risk" youth they are designed to benefit; at present, she is examining a mentoring program for middle school girls. Levy has conducted research with UVa's Partnership for Leaders in Education, and is co-author of several articles on school turnaround. Prior to earning her master's degree in education from the University of Virginia, she served as a middle school band director in Fairfax County, Virginia and as

American University Hillel's program director. Levy earned a bachelor's degree in music education from Indiana University.

Stephen A. Saunders has been a French, English, and photography teacher, and award-winning soccer coach, for nearly a decade. He currently is a doctoral student in educational administration and supervision at the University of Virginia's Curry School of Education, where he also serves as Curry's supervisor of administrative interns in schools across Virginia. While working with UVa's Partnership for Leaders in Education, he conducted fieldwork in a number of schools undergoing the "turnaround" process. Saunders earned a bachelor's degree in political science, French, and public service from Hampden-Sydney College, and master's degrees in both French language and administration and supervision from the University of Virginia.